Walking t
Isles of Mull, Iona, Coll and Tiree

Publisher's Note

Producing this volume gives the sort of quiet satisfaction felt when fitting the last piece into a difficult jig-saw puzzle. There are of course more volumes to come in the Walking Scotland Series, but this one completes the pattern of the inner Scottish islands, enabling us to offer recently-published or revised guides to every accessible island from Arran and Islay to Skye.

It is good to have here the result of our authors' comprehensive exploration of the Isle of Mull, which has become one of the most popular off-shore objectives for active visitors, and which has so much to offer them in its variety of scenic beauty and adventure opportunities.

Mull and Iona are grouped in this volume with Coll and Tiree, which lie quite close to the west and are clearly visible from their bigger neighbour. Sadly, the days when the Coll/Tiree boat called at Tobermory pier are but a fond memory. With careful timing, it is quite feasible to visit all the islands in this book on the same trip, but you have to go back to Oban and start again.

In all volumes of the WALKING SCOTLAND series, the authors make every effort to ensure accuracy, but changes can occur after publication. Reports of such changes are welcomed by the publisher. Neither the publisher nor the authors can accept responsibility for errors, omissions or any loss or injury.

Location Map

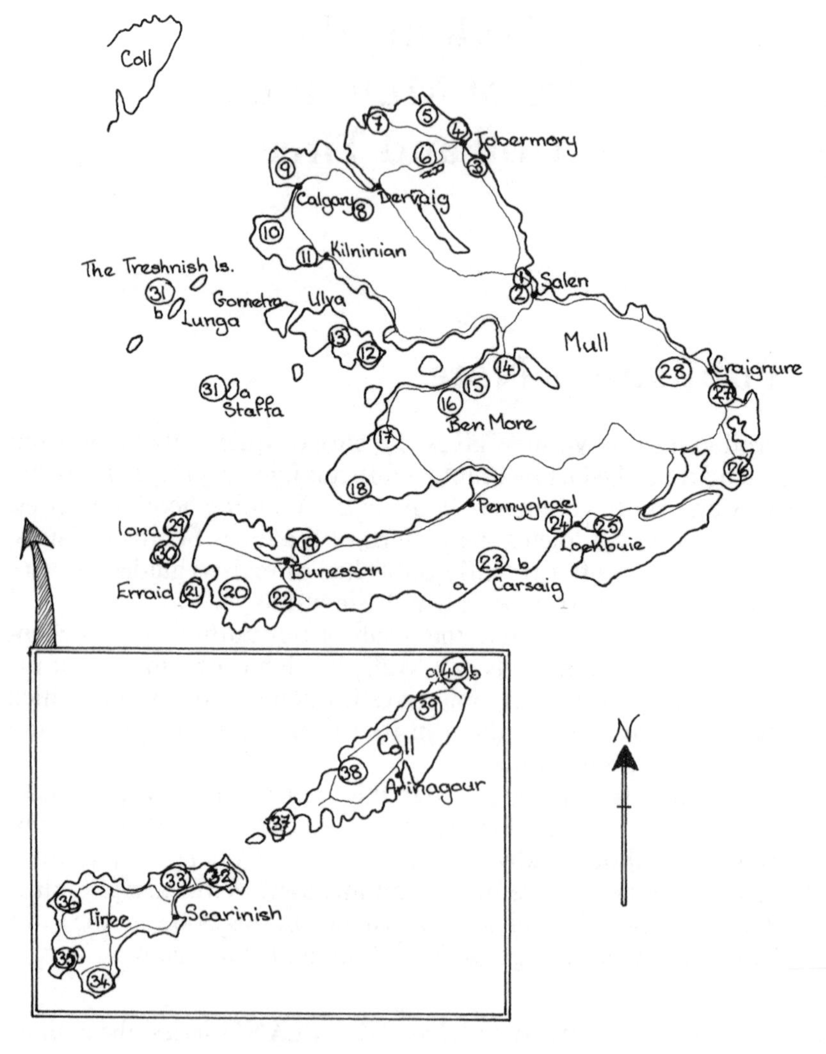

Clan Walk Guides

Walking the Isles of Mull, Iona, Coll and Tiree

Walking Scotland Series

Volume 10

Mary Welsh

and

Christine Isherwood

First published by Clan Books, 2008
Incorporating chapters originally published under the title
Walks on Tiree, Coll, Colonsay and a Taste of Mull
by Westmorland Gazette, 1996

ISBN 978 1 873597 15 6

Clan Books
Clandon House
The Cross, Doune
Perthshire
FK16 6BE

Typeset by Rowland Phototypesetting Ltd,
Bury St Edmunds, Suffolk
Printed and bound in Great Britain by
St Edmundsbury Press Ltd, Bury St Edmunds, Suffolk

Contents

Contents continued page 4

The Authors' Golden Rules for Good, Safe Walking

- Wear suitable clothes and take adequate waterproofs.
- Walk in strong footwear; walking boots are advisable.
- Carry the relevant map and a compass and know how to use them.
- Carry a whistle; remember six long blasts repeated at one minute intervals is the distress signal.
- Do not walk alone, and tell someone where you are going.
- If mist descends, return.
- Keep all dogs under strict control. Observe all "No Dogs" notices – they are there for very good reasons.

1

Glenaros from Salen

Park in the parking area just before the bus shelter at Salen, grid ref 572433. This lies on the shore side of the road, on the north edge of village, on the A848, 10 miles/14.4km south-east of Tobermory.

The stark ruins of the 13th century **Aros Castle** stand on a high bluff, with wonderful strategic views over the Sound of Mull and Salen Bay. It was built by the MacDougalls and was once one of several castles guarding the Sound. In 1608, Hebridean chiefs were invited to the castle. They were later asked to dine on the flagship *Moon*, belonging to Lord Ochiltree, the Lieutenant of the Isles. Once they had finished their meal, they were kidnapped and imprisoned for nearly a year in various places in Scotland, until they had sworn loyalty to the House of Stuart.

Aros Old Bridge

1 From the parking area walk along the A848, in the direction of Tobermory, for a ¼ mile/0.5km, facing the oncoming traffic. Then cross and take a kissing gate beside a gate, which bears a notice 'No dogs'. Climb gently, ascending a pleasing track through deciduous woodland. When the trees cease on your right, enjoy the glorious view over the Sound to Beinn Hiant on Ardnamurchan on the mainland. Pass through a gate and walk on beside a wall on your left, with a dramatic view of the castle to your right. Continue on, keeping to the left of Glenaros House, to join a narrow metalled access road. Turn right and descend to cross the A848.

2 Bear left over a green sward and then, before the road bridge, drop down under trees on a narrow path to cross the picturesque old stone bridge spanning the Aros River. Turn right, pass in front of two cottages and walk on along the continuing track that edges the lovely river, where you are likely to see mergansers, eiders and the occasional goosander. Pass below the ruins of the castle and press on beyond towards the White House of Aros, at one time an inn. Beyond, the delightful way ends at a small pier. Return along the track and take the first right turn.

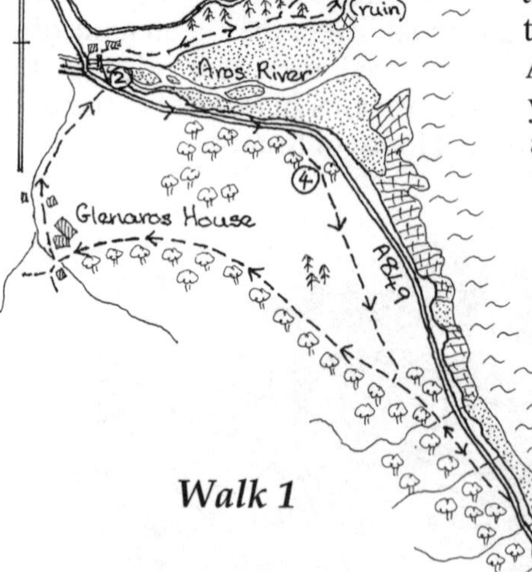

3 Climb the slope through trees to the ruins, which lie to your left, beyond a gate. Bear left across a grassy swathe and climb a stile to the foot of the castle walls and walk right. Enjoy the ruins but remember to observe the warning about their dangerous state. Then drop down from the castle by a narrow path leading, right, away from the ruins. Descend an easy way through a glorious bluebell woodland to rejoin the track beside the river. Turn right and walk on until you can cross the old stone bridge once more. Climb the slope, turn left, and cross the A-road when you reach the telephone box. Continue along the road, with care, for 400yds/370m, and then take the second track, leading off right.

4 Climb the pleasing way, over pasture, passing through two gates, and at the boundary wall, walk right to join the footpath taken earlier. Turn left to retrace your outward route through the fine deciduous woodland to the road. Turn right to return to the parking area.

Goosanders

Practicals

Type of walk: Full of interest but please note that the ruins are in a precarious state.

Total Distance: 4½ miles/7.2km
Time: 2½ hours
Maps: OS Explorer 374/Landranger 47

2

Salen and Cnoc na Sroine hillfort

Park as for walk 1.

Salen was founded by General Lachlan MacQuarrie, who, it is believed, was born at Ormaig on the south side of Ulva, when his parents moved there from Mull. After a brilliant career in the army he became the first Governor of Australia's New South Wales. He eventually returned to Mull and when he died in 1824, was interred in the mausoleum at Gruline, 2 miles south–west of Salen.

1 Walk along the A-road, in the direction of Tobermory, facing the on-coming traffic, for ¼ mile/0.5km. Cross and take the metal

Cnoc na Sroine (hillfort)

kissing gate into deciduous woodland and climb gently. When the trees cease, carry on along the gated path continuing ahead until you reach the metalled access road to Glenaros House and the farm, on your right, and then, to your left, 'Kate's Cottage'. Ignore both dwellings and cross the road to go ahead through a metal gate. Wind round left on a track, with the wall to your left. Where the wall turns away, left, go straight ahead on the rough track out onto the moorland slopes.

2 Where the track becomes indistinct, keep ahead over a grassy area, climb a little and then go on where the track emerges once more. Follow the distinct way as it contours a short way, around the side of a low hillock, to your left. Ford the burn, Allt a' Chaisteil, to continue climbing gently. Keep left of a boggy patch in the track and then return to the main track and go on, steadily ascending towards the hill ahead, Cnoc na Sroine, crowned with a hillfort. Just after another boggy patch, engulfing the track, look towards the hill, now on your left, to see two grassy paths climbing the slopes (made by walkers and cows).

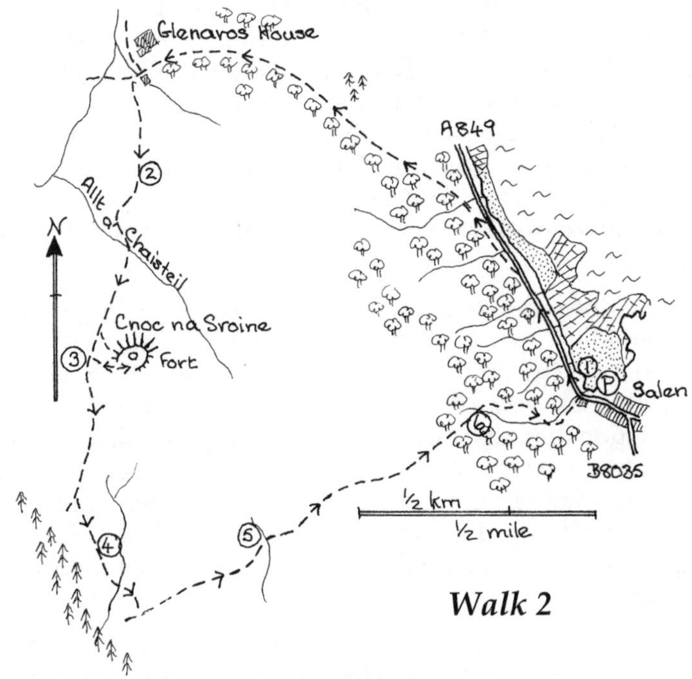

Walk 2

Curlew

3 Take the one to the right, which is the easier, to attain the top. Near the summit, follow the path as it curves round, left of the ramparts and then go through a gap in the ruined wall into a large hollow grassy area surrounded with more wall. On the far side is a cairn. From here you can see, left, Loch Frisa, and ahead, over the Sound of Mull to Morvern. To the south-west lies Loch na Keal. Return from the hilltop by your upward route and turn left to continue. Divert round the next boggy patch and continue to the brow. Here the track becomes grassy and indistinct. Wind round right with a couple of cairns on your right, above on rocks, to help you. Then the track emerges, still rather peaty, and begins to descend towards distant conifers. Go on down a more distinct way now with the conifers well away to your right.

4 Keep on down the clearer narrow path, passing a large clump of birch and low-growing willow. Follow it as it turns a little left and crosses a stream to go on through sweet-smelling bog myrtle and with a last view of Loch na Keal to your right. On reaching a T-junction of paths, turn left and in a few steps, detour left, and then right, to avoid a very boggy patch. Pass through a clump of birch and wind left and then right again, as other walkers have, to avoid more bog. The path continues and each time it becomes boggy follow the diversions used by others. (The in-between bits are delightful!)

5 Then the birch is left behind and you reach a rather extensive area of bog about a stream. Here climb left before attempting to cross, as other ramblers have done. Join the main path once more and walk on the improving path as it continues over the shoulder of Braigh a' Choire Mhoir, from where curlews call. Once over the brow you can spot Salen far below. Stride on beside the fence, now on your right, soon to move into deciduous woodland. Descend the path through the trees, where you will have to divert to avoid blown down trees. When the path divides, choose either as both paths come together at a low fence, which you step over or climb it beside a broken stile.

6 Go on down the clear path, avoiding wet patches and follow it through a short stretch of head-high bracken. Finally you can spot the old church (now a private house) through the trees. The path becomes indistinct but keep heading towards the dwelling. Step over a wire fence and drop down a little path, curving left, to join an access track and then the A-road. Turn right and walk a few yards to the parking area.

Heath milkwort

Practicals

Type of walk: This is a challenging route and you must be prepared for boggy areas after rain. But the fort is dramatic, the views are excellent and the feeling of being up on wide open moorland is exhilarating.

Total Distance: 5 miles/8km
Time: 3 hours
Maps: OS Explorer 374/Landranger 47

3

Aros Park, Tobermory

Park in the large Ledaig Car Park at the bottom of the hill, on the right, just past the distillery, grid ref 505551. To access this use the A848, going north, into Tobermory.

Lower Fall, Aros Park

Mink

Aros House stood on the site of the car park crossed during this walk. It was built by the Allan family, shipowners of Liverpool. The house was demolished in 1962, but its policies, now managed by the Forestry Commission, form a fine public park.

Mink farms were started in Britain in 1929. Some mink have escaped, and you might see one here. They are a little larger than a stoat, very dark brown, sometimes with a white throat patch.

1 From the car park walk past the pub and restaurant. Take the small signed path, with an information board at its start, to climb a short way up the end of the cliff. Then continue along a shelf with the sea below to the left and a vegetated cliff to the right, the beautiful path passing through oak, beech and hazel, with banks of woodrush. Cross a burn, just before it plunges over the cliff to the sea below in a glorious waterfall called the Sput Dubh (Black Spout). It was used by ships, in the past, to take on fresh water. Turn right before a barrier that closes the old path where it has landslipped and is also blocked by many fallen trees. Climb steps up through a shallow valley to the cliff top and then follow the path inside a fence, with fields to the right. The way then re-enters woodland, where you should ignore a path to the right, signed 'Main Driveway', and carry on above the sea to descend steps. Continue along the path to cross a

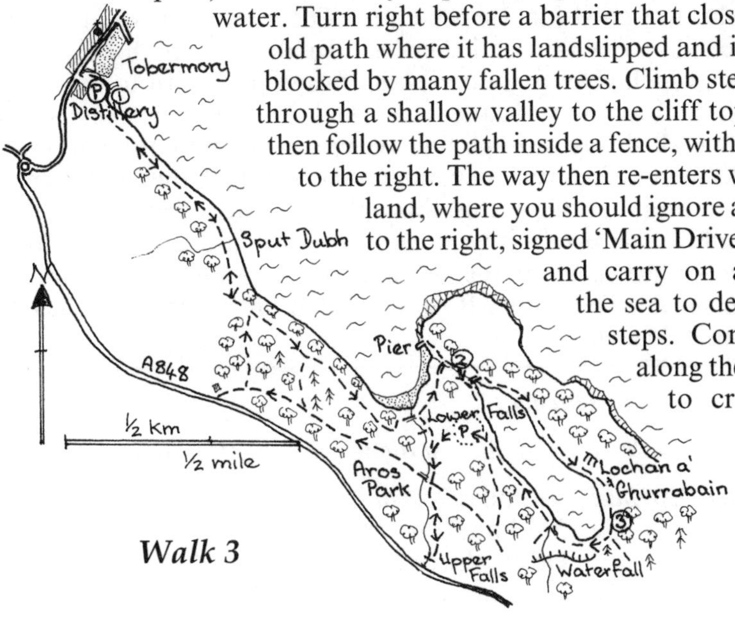

Walk 3

tiny burn beside a pool, and descend by zigzags and more steps to rejoin the original route. Cross the large burn below a fine waterfall and carry on past a right turn, following signs for the pier. Come down to join a track at a T-junction, where, if you wish, you can turn left to the pier to view Tobermory across the bay, otherwise turn right.

2 Go past some buildings and take the left turn at the Y -junction. Cross the outflow from Lochan Ghurrabain and continue along the right branch of the track, which runs along the shore under fine beeches. Look for dabchicks and mallards on the water among the waterlilies, which are at their best in summer. In the distance, high up above the far side of the lochan, there is a dramatic waterfall coming over a cliff into the valley.

3 Take the right hand path at the end of the lochan, keeping by the waterside. Then go right again at a ruined pump-house and carry on above the shore. On reaching a boathouse, bear left and go up the bank, and on to a large car park. Go ahead towards a toilet block and, beyond, pick up a green track. Fork left, as soon as you can, to climb gently uphill. Turn left at the next T-junction and walk up beside the delightful cascading burn until you reach the main driveway. Cross, and take the continuing path beside the burn, signed for 'Upper Falls'. These are most spectacular, especially after rain and there is a small rocky path off to the right, which gives a good view halfway up. Return to the main path, go back down to the tarmacked drive. Turn left and stroll the metalled way through fine mature woodland until you reach a gate across the drive. Beyond it, take a path on the right, signed 'Tobermory'. Follow this through pleasant woods and down a flight of steps to join your outward path along the cliff. You may see herons along the shore, and keep a look out for mink, especially in Tobermory Bay, where they are attracted by the fish being unloaded.

Practicals

Type of walk: Lots of interest along the delightful route.

Total Distance: 4½ miles/7.4km
Time: 2–3 hours
Maps: OS Explorer 374/Landranger 47

4

Tobermory to the lighthouse at Rubha nan Gall

Park in the free Ledaig car park, close to the harbour, at the southern end of Tobermory, grid ref 505551 (as for walk 3).

Tobermory is the capital of Mull and the only town. It is located in the north east of the island, its houses lining a very sheltered bay. It was founded in 1788 for the British Fisheries Society and two hundred years before this a Spanish Galleon, part of the routed Armada, sought shelter in the Bay. She was said to have 3 million gold doubloons on board. After two uneasy months, the ship sank when Donald Glass Maclean, who

Rubha nan Gall

had been held prisoner, managed to ignite the gunpowder store. Many salvage attempts have been made but many think the bulk of the treasure is still buried on the bottom of the bay.

Walk 4

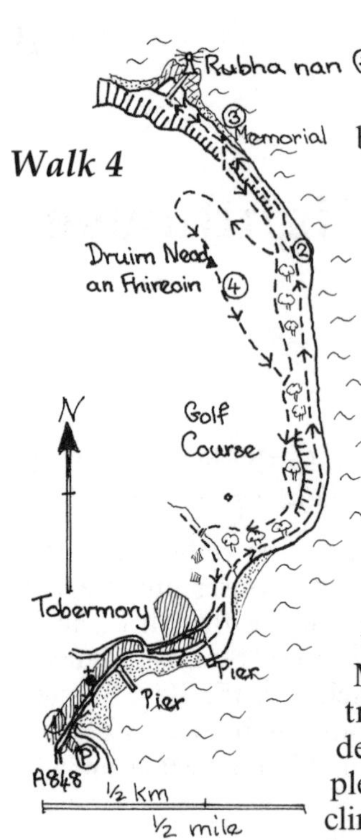

The brightly coloured houses that line the gracefully curving bay of Tobermory give the walker a warm welcome. The town's name means '**Well of Mary**' though it is uncertain now where the well is. Allow yourself time to enjoy the many small shops before you set off to the lighthouse, Rubha nan Gall and the hill of Druim Nead an Fhireoin.

1 From the car park wind round to walk the Main Street to Caledonian MacBrayne's pier and take the reinforced track, which ascends steadily through deciduous woodland. Continue on the pleasing high-level way. Wooded slopes climb steeply above you and drop steeply to the shore. Parts of this path require careful walking. Follow the path as it emerges from the trees and on along the cliffs, with a magnificent view of the Sound of Mull, Loch Sunart, and Morvern on the Mainland.

2 Keep on the lower path as it descends through more birch to come to a memorial to Robert John Brown of Tobermory. Sit on the seat and use the viewfinder to identify the breathtaking scene. Then walk on to the lighthouse, Rubha nan Gall, now fitted with solar panels. It was automated in the 1960s, a hundred years after it was built. If you wish to walk any further, perhaps round to see Bloody Bay, you need to go down on the shore and through the arch which carries the lighthouse path. Here you might see cormorants flying just above the waves.

3 Return to the steep rough track, known as Jacob's Ladder, which leaves the main path on the right close to the memorial. Then climb to a division of tracks through the bracken, where you take the right branch. Bear right to pass on your left, several ruined houses. Then take the first track left, which leads to the cairn on Druim Nead an Fhireoin, 280ft/86m. Enjoy this superb view-point, from where you can see Calve Island, which guards the entrance to Tobermory Bay and makes it a safe anchorage.

4 Stroll the clear path, south, along the top and descend over heather moorland to rejoin the path you left earlier. Follow the way as it swings right towards a stile over a sturdy fence onto Tobermory golf course. Here a notice welcomes walkers 'at their own risk', and you are asked to follow the marker posts, keep to the side of the fairways, and avoid disrupting play. The posts do take you on a delightful route around the edge of the course and bring you eventually through an iron gate onto a track. Bear left and follow it round right to join a metalled road, where you turn left. Pass the war memorial and stride on. At the road junction, turn left and then rejoin Main Street to return to your car.

Cormorant

Practicals

Type of walk: Easy pleasing walking. Path through woods can be muddy after rain. Jacob's Ladder is quite steep and can be wet.

Total Distance:	2½ miles/4km
Time:	2 hours
Maps:	OS Explorer 374/Landranger 47

5

Ardmore Bay

Park in the Forestry Commission's parking area on the edge of Ardmore Forest, grid ref 485559. This is reached from Tobermory by taking the Dervaig road, B8073. After ¼ mile/0.5km, take the right turn for Glengorm. A mile along, turn right onto a forest road where the parking area lies against the edge of the forest.

With the harvesting of the timber more and more ruined cottages are emerging from the understorey. At **Penalbanach** several sad cottages and a two storey house stand to the right of

Ruined house, Penalbanach

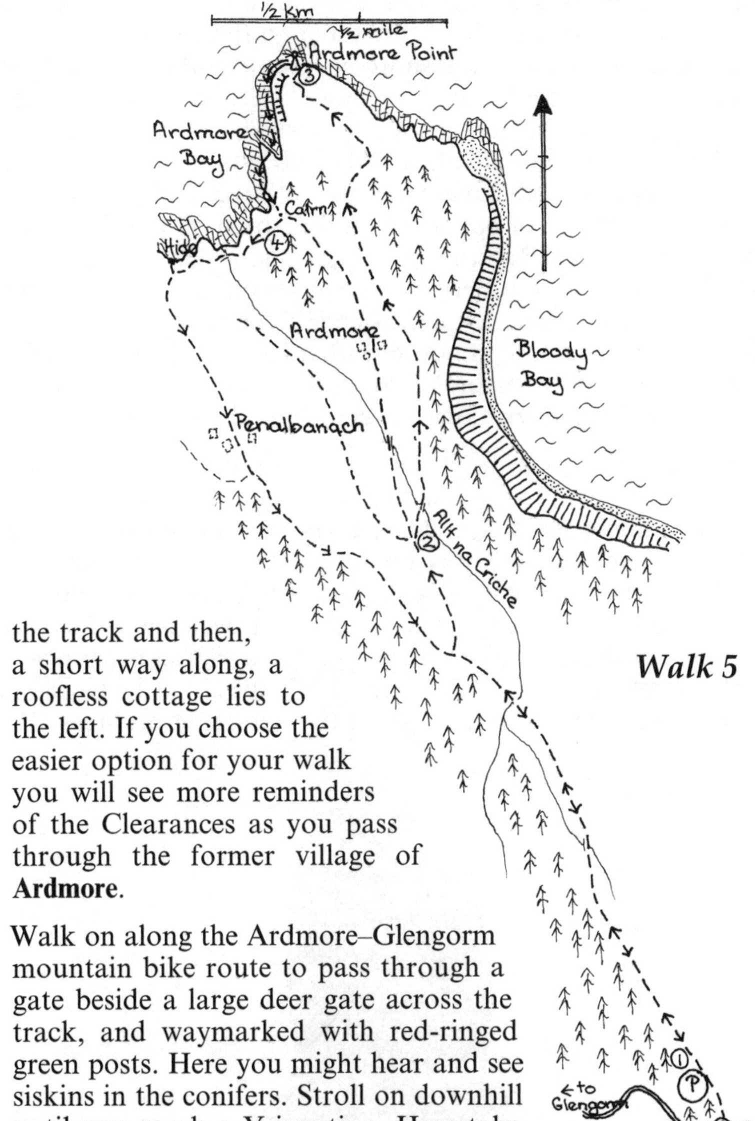

Walk 5

the track and then, a short way along, a roofless cottage lies to the left. If you choose the easier option for your walk you will see more reminders of the Clearances as you pass through the former village of **Ardmore**.

1 Walk on along the Ardmore–Glengorm mountain bike route to pass through a gate beside a large deer gate across the track, and waymarked with red-ringed green posts. Here you might hear and see siskins in the conifers. Stroll on downhill until you reach a Y-junction. Here take the right branch to pass through large areas of clear-fell from where you can view the end of the Ardnamurchan peninsula and maybe the ferry 'ploughing' up the Sound of Mull. After 1½ miles/2.5km you are confronted by several tracks.

2 Ignore the left turn and the one going ahead; the latter takes you by track and path to the picnic table on the viewpoint and the bird hide, both above the shore of Ardmore Bay, avoiding the challenging clamber along the shore. This walk uses the track leading off right, which is not waymarked. Follow the track on and on, bearing right uphill, and then go with it as it winds round left. When you reach a really wet place on the track, about a mile from the junction of paths, take a little path on the right, made by other walkers. Return to the track and go on winding round until the track ends. Carry on along the continuing narrow path and then drop, right, down the steepish grassy slopes, to the very modern automated lighthouse, with a battery of solar panels to power the light for Ardmore Point. Keep a look out here for sea eagles which can sometimes be seen along the coast.

3 Leave the lighthouse on its left side, west, by descending a little gully almost next to the building to reach a short stretch of path – which alas soon fades. Then carry on well above the shore along a rough pathless way up against the foot of the very high cliffs, where you have to push your way through the rampant vegetation. Or you may prefer to clamber over the rocks on the shore. Continue on along the shore for a few steps to reach a dyke, a long ridge of rock, running askew across the beach and out to sea. Keep to the sea side of this for better progress. Then

Sea eagle

climb a small gully that is naturally stepped to ascend a low cliff. Walk on to see a large reed bed below. Descend over rocks and push through a short patch of reeds and then go on along the edge of the bed to come to a better path, where you can stride out. Descend a short gully, with rocks to help you down onto a beach, where there are two large cairns and from where you can spot a red ringed post once more; this is where the track, now a path, ignored earlier, joins the shore.

4 Carry on the distinct path, through bracken, which curves round one of the inlets of the bay. Climb sturdy wooden steps that take you up onto a low cliff to walk on through more bracken to arrive at a picnic table set on a good viewpoint, where you will want to pause. Head on to go over a little bridge and then climb more strong wooden steps to wind round the hilltop fort of An Dunan. Continue over several duckboards and wind slightly right to reach the bird hide from where you may see seals, cormorants and many oystercatchers. After a pause, leave the hut and walk straight ahead along a delightful green path through clear-fell and sometimes with conifers away to the left or the right. Pass between the ruined cottages of Penalbanach and soon join the forest ride, where you turn left to return to the parking area.

Practicals

Type of walk: Most of the way is on forest roads, rides and a grassy path. The route from the lighthouse to the cairns at Ardmore Bay is challenging. Take it slowly and carefully and the ½ mile/1km will be completed and enjoyed. If you do not want to attempt this part, you could return from the lighthouse to the first acute right turn and then follow the track and path to reach the Bay or miss out the lighthouse altogether.

Total Distance:	5½ mile/9km
Time:	3 hours
Maps:	OS Explorer 374/Landranger 47

6

'S Airde Beinn and Crater Loch

Park just before a roofless cottage, on the right, where there is room for two cars, grid ref 475526. To reach this, drive the B8073 from Tobermory for about 3 miles/5km. If this space is unavailable, return along the road for 110yds/100m to park in a large space in an old quarry, on the same side of the road.

'S Airde Beinn means 'high hill' but don't let that translation put you off. It is not very high and it is delightful to climb, with wonderful views awaiting you from the top and the superb deep Lochan 'S Airde Beinn, or Crater Loch, cradled in the hollow below.

1 Climb the stile over the fence from the parking area beside the cottage. Follow the path that climbs slightly left and then uphill through bracken and willow to reach a gate. Beyond take the

'S Airde Beinn

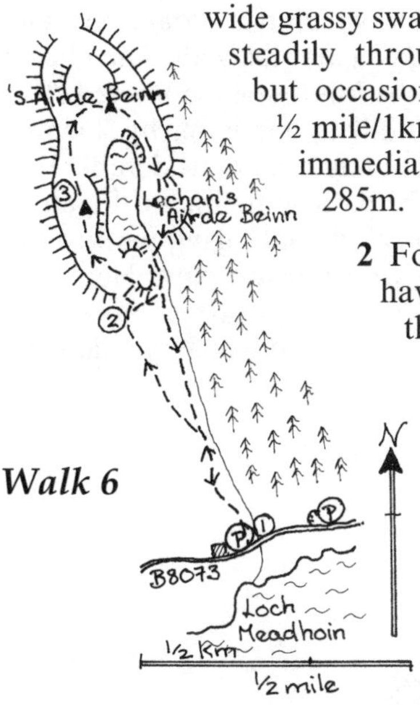

wide grassy swathe that bears off half left and climb steadily through heather. The path is distinct but occasionally the peaty base is soft. After ½ mile/1km the path comes to the foot of the immediate high ground, cairned at 922ft/ 285m.

Walk 6

2 Follow the clear path, where ramblers have walked before, as it winds left and then begins to climb easily to the rim of the crater of the ancient volcano. Carry on around the rim from where you can look down on the loch that fills the great hollow – delightfully blue on a lovely sunny day. There are wonderful views across the crater to the Sound of Mull and Ardnamurchan. As you go on you reach a cairn, the highest point of 'S Airde Beinn, 959ft/ 292m, where you will want to pause to see the islands of Rum and Eigg, now in view.

3 Carry on all round the rim, from where skylarks rise, passing another cairn and going over and around some very easy rocks. Follow the distinct path, which eventually descends to a wall. Pass through a convenient gap and turn left. Keep beside a little

Skylark

stream, the outflow from the lochan, which has broken through the crater rim. It descends between you and the wall. Then begin to curve, right, round the foot of the hill first encountered. It is possible to follow this path downhill to the gate, by keeping parallel with the stream, but if there has been considerable rain the ground will be very soft and the path sometimes difficult to spot. If so it is better to keep on a small contouring path round the base of the hill until you reach your upward path. Here turn left and retrace your earlier steps over the heather moorland. Both paths come together at the gate, beyond which you descend to the parking area.

Whinchat

Practicals

Type of walk: A lovely ramble if the ground is not too wet to walk to the foot of the hill. The rim of the crater is superb.

Total Walk: 2–3 miles/3.1–5km
Time: 1½ hours
Maps: OS Explorer 374/Landranger 47

Dun Ara and Dun Ban, Glen Gorm

Walkers are welcome to park in the large car park by the coffee shop, grid ref 441572. To access this, take the B8073, signed for Dervaig and Calgary, from Tobermory. After ½km take the right fork for Glengorm. The surface at the time of writing is quite potholed, so drive with care. Four miles along the road go through imposing white-painted gates and immediately take the right fork to the car park by the excellent coffee shop (closed in winter).

Glengorm Castle was built by James Forsyth, who became owner of the Quinish and Glengorm (at that time called Sorne) estates in 1847. By various devious means he removed the crofters and demolished their homes to make room for his mansion, which he intended to call Dunara. An old woman suggested Glengorm (blue glen) instead and he was delighted with

Dun Ara

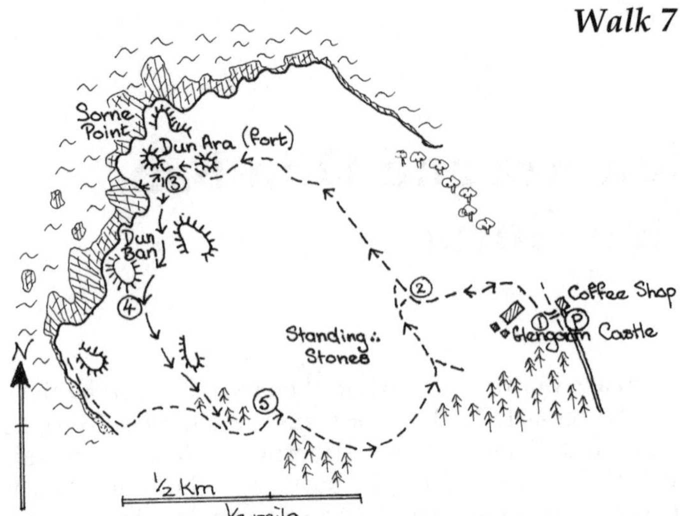

the name; so was she, because to her it was a reminder that the glen had been blue with the smoke from the burning houses. It is said that one of the evicted crofters cursed Forsyth, saying that he would never sleep in his new house, and indeed he became ill and died soon after the castle was finished and before he had moved in.

Dun Ara occupies a superb defensive position on a steep rocky bastion beside Sorne Point. The ruins are mediaeval and some obvious stonework remains; they probably stand on the site of an older structure. It is likely to have belonged to the MacKinnons, who controlled the lands of Mishnish until they were ousted by the MacLeans in the 17th Century.

The **bathing pool** is said to have been adapted as such for the Lithgows, the shipping family, who owned Glengorm at one time. Previously it may have been a harbour for Dun Ara; look for signs of a jetty.

1 Walk across in front of the coffee shop and then turn left to cross a bridge over a lower track. Wind right, following signs for Dun Ara, Bathing Pool and Standing Stones. The track runs between rhododendrons to a gate into pasture. Carry on along a clear well-made grassy track across the pasture, with the imposing Scots baronial pile of Glengorm castle above to the left, and a superb view across to Ardnamurchan with Rum behind it to the right.

2 Go through a gate and take the grassy right branch, which runs along beside the fence. Cross a stony track and go over a stile between two gates, then continue on the grassy way down the next field. Cross the stile, or use the gate, into the next field; this one is rather wet but by walking on the higher ground to the right of the track all difficulties can be avoided. Head round to the left for the next gate, after which there is a waymark. The track winds round through basalt outcrops, with a spectacular rocky coastline beyond, and Coll and Tiree in the distance. Then ahead on the edge of the shore is an isolated rocky eminence, which is Dun Ara. Follow a path leading up the lower part of the outcrop, then climb up a rocky basalt staircase to the summit. The walls of the dun remain, and another low building. It is not vitrified. The view from the top is magnificent.

3 Return to the track and follow it down to the shore and the bathing pool, where you might like to take a break. Then go back to the track, below the dun again, and take a small path on the right (straight ahead if coming down from the dun), to go across a bridge of sleepers to a gate. Beyond, continue up a faint path which winds round the edge of the slope above, heading for the next basalt outcrop which is Dun Ban. Leave the path and head right towards Dun Ban, cross a tiny burn in a hollow, and then go up the far side towards another gate. Go through into the field and circle round above the fence. You can only view the dun, not visit.

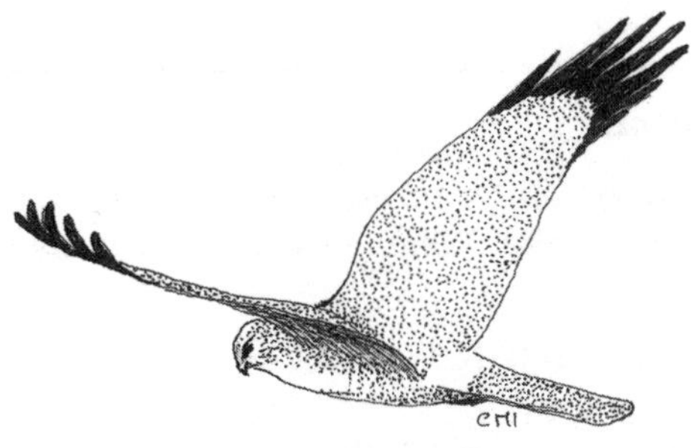

Hen harrier

4 To continue, keep to the edge of the higher ground and walk inland towards a small wood. Go through a gate at the top of the wood and take the rough track down through the edge of the trees to a reinforced track 25yds/20m further on, where you turn left. Look for hen harriers all about this area in winter, and you may also see kestrels and buzzards.

5 The track crosses a low col and then turns right. Go through a gate and on through a conifer plantation, then wind left, pass through another gate and climb steadily uphill. Ignore the right turn and continue on round the hillside. Look left to see three standing stones in a ring of small stones; you can walk over the field to inspect them at closer quarters. Then return to the track and walk on. At the Y-junction take the right branch and follow it round to rejoin your outward path to return to the car park.

Kestrel

Practicals

Type of walk: A lovely ramble through spectacular rocky scenery, with a fine dun and standing stones to visit, and it ends at a coffee shop.

Total Distance:	3 miles/5km
Time:	2–3 hours
Maps:	OS Explorer 374/Landranger 47

8

Cille a'Mhoraire

Park in the small car park for the Ardhu Community Woodland on the right hand side of the road grid ref 428499. To access this take the B8073 west from Tobermory to Dervaig. About ½ mile/ 1km beyond Dervaig, turn left onto a minor road signed Torloisk, also to the Old Byre Heritage Centre (which has an excellent café and much interesting information).

There are many **ruined villages** like Cille a'Mhoraire, Mary's Cell or Church, on Mull, remnants of the infamous clearances, when the crofters were turned off their land to make way for

Ford and waterfall, Kengharair

sheep. Often the houses were burned, but in some places the well-built walls are still standing. Notice the rounded corners, typical of these cottages. They would have been black houses, built without any mortar in the walls and roofed with heather thatch.

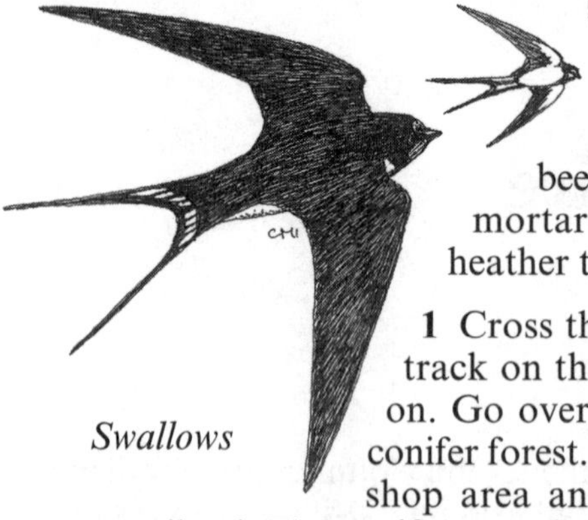

Swallows

1 Cross the road and walk right to take a track on the left a few yards/metres farther on. Go over a cattle grid and walk into the conifer forest. Soon the track goes past a workshop area and then runs on into pleasanter woodland. The conifers recede and the track is lined with hazel, bearing nuts in summer and autumn. Carry on until you come out of the woodland into pastures. Head on towards Kengharair Farm, where swallows swoop round the buildings in summer. Just before the gate to the farmhouse turn left on a track, which runs below its garden, past a fine tall elm tree, and then continues past an outbuilding at the end of which you bear left. Go through a gate, cross a field and through a second gate to ford a burn with a small waterfall below it, and surrounded by mature trees. Here you may see grey wagtails. The track winds on downhill in zigzags to the valley bottom and continues along it, through very pleasant open country.

2 Stroll on to cross the Allt Coille Chill' a' Mhoraire on basalt shelves, if the water is low, but it has some big irregular stepping stones for times of spate. Beyond, go into a birch wood and on past a cattle feeding station, where it could be very muddy in winter, and then out of the wood into more pasture.

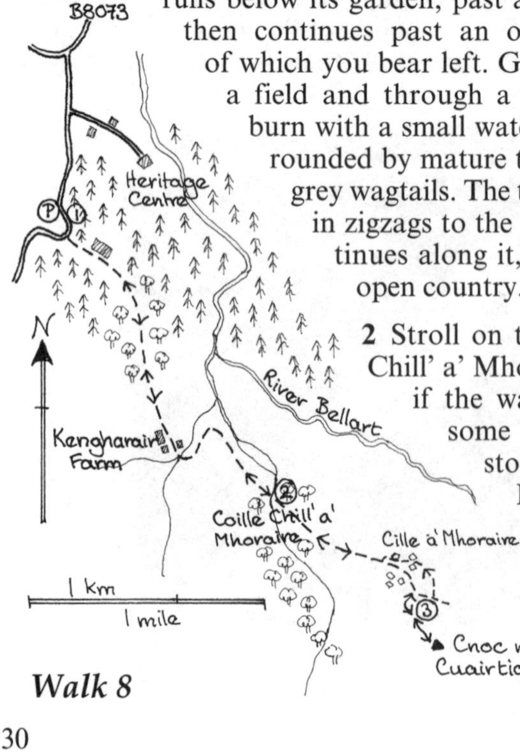

Walk 8

The path winds round little basalt hillocks; look across to the hillside on your right to see the lava layers, with stripes of woodland along them. As the track climbs more steeply between the rocky knolls, look left to see the first of the ruined houses in the old village of Cille a'Mhoraire. Climb to the end of the reinforced track and look among the bracken where you will find many remains of houses and byres. Head right up a grassy track and then take animal paths which lead through the bracken onto the ridge of Cnoc na Cuairtich, the hill which sheltered the village from the south, and on up to the top. There is a higher hill behind if you are feeling energetic, but this little one still gives a fine view back down the valley to Dervaig, with its conspicuous white church spire, and the sea.

3 Return to the end of the reinforced track and carry on, above the fence, on a vague path. Go through the field gate at the end of the fence and turn sharply left to come back down the field where more ruined houses are cradled in a sheltered hollow. Then walk left round a knoll to look at the biggest one still standing, with its characteristic rounded wall corners. Leave the field by a gate below this ruin, turn right on the track and retrace your steps to the farm and then your car.

Practicals

Type of walk: An easy gentle walk on a track through woodland and pastures. The views are pleasant rather than spectacular. There could be difficulty fording the Allt Coille Chill a'Mhoraire after heavy rain, in spite of the stepping stones which are rather irregular. The track may also be muddy beyond this if the farmer has been feeding his cows there. The cows themselves appear to be shy of people and moved away, but it would not be wise to take a dog.

Total Distance:	5 miles/8km.Add another mile if you wish to climb the hill.
Time:	2–3 hours
Maps:	OS Explorer 374/Landranger 47

9

Calgary Bay and Caliach Point

Park in the car park by the beach, grid ref 373 513, or if that is full use a smaller one opposite the Calgary Hotel, grid ref 378 517. There is also space on the grass for car parking at the end of the minor road to Calaich, grid ref 357 538, if you are using two cars or being picked up. This minor road leaves the B8073 at the top of the hill down to Calgary, before you reach the hotel; there is a house on the corner but no signpost. To access Calgary use the B8073, which runs round the north of Mull from Tobermory. Calgary is about 5 miles west of Dervaig.

Calgary Bay has one of the few sandy beaches on Mull, which is backed by dunes and fertile grassland known as machair. The latter supports a wide variety of plants and it is at risk here. Over the years, winds and waves have worn away the machair face. Rabbit burrows, grazing sheep, car tracks, tramping feet have all made this erosion worse. In September 1993 Argyll Conservation Volunteers started work using various methods to slow down the erosion. Little fences were erected and

Calgary Bay

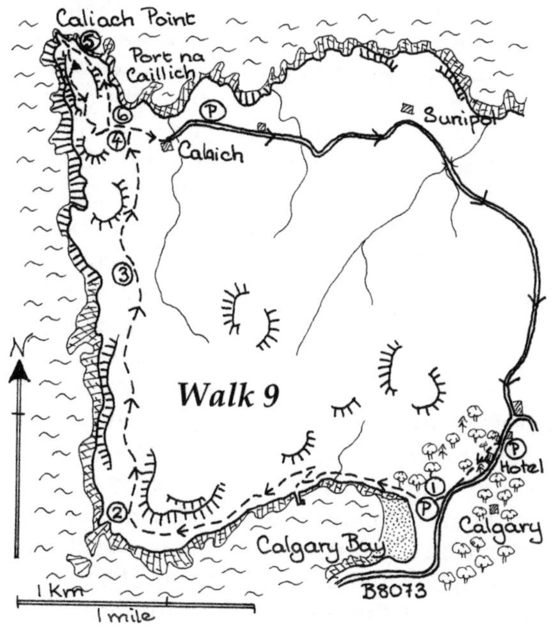

have helped rebuild the dunes, while turf boxes and marram grass planting keeps the sand in place, stopping the edge of the machair from being undermined in places, and preventing it from collapsing. Fences have been constructed to protect planted areas and to keep animals (and humans) out.

The name **cailleach** means old woman. A legend is told that once an old woman was cut off by the tide whilst she was out collecting shellfish, but she managed to climb up the cliff to safety. However instead of giving thanks for her escape she boasted of her cleverness, and as a punishment was turned into a rock standing in the bay below the Point.

You pass the **corn-drying kiln** as you go up to the old village from the seat. It is a stone-lined hollow in the side of a small hill, about 4ft/1.2m deep and probably a similar width at the top, narrowing to 1½ft/0.5m at the base. There is a hole with a lintel at the base. A fire would have been lit in the bottom and the corn, barley or oats spread on hazel branches laid across, above it, until it was dry, or sometimes even singed. Then it could be winnowed and ground.

1 Walk on from the car park towards the beach, then along the track, which runs on the north side of the bay. Go through a kissing gate beside a gate, signposted 'Calaich 6km.' Carry on through woodland above the shore, then out onto open ground until you reach a pink granite pier. The track turns right here and runs uphill through a gate to reach three gates all together with a building off to the right. Go through the left gate and walk up a path, which runs beside the fence. At the top bear left onto the 100ft/30m wave-cut platform and walk round the edge. Then move inland to cross a burn and go through a gate just beyond. Follow the good path, which winds round the edge of the platform again; this time it comes inland to a stile with a sign 'Calaich 2¾ miles/4.5km'. Go over the stile and along the path, now much narrower and rockier, as it winds through bracken beside a fenced geo. At the far side of the cleft the path widens out again. Go though an area of large boulders, which have fallen from the basalt cliffs above, and then past a large vertical stone (visible from Calgary Beach). Carry on slightly downhill to cross a bracken covered area to the end of the headland where Calgary Bay reaches the sea, and the path turns the corner.

2 Go through an old stone wall and turn right to walk beside it. There are dramatic crags above and a wide level flat cut into them which was once inhabited; there are walls, remains of buildings, cultivation ridges, and many paths. Keep straight ahead, and enjoy the lovely views out to Coll and Tiree. Climb a small raise and walk ahead towards a line of low crags with a cave; head for a break in the cliffs to the right of the cave and go up it to a post with a bright green top. From here you can see another green-topped post some distance away; make for it. There is no definite path and there is a defile to negotiate, best crossed towards its inland end. Then head for a hill with an extraordinary crown of rock on top and walk the clear path winding round below it. Make your way over easy ground to the next post on a small rise some distance ahead.

3 Walk on to the next post on a higher hill and then descend to a gate in a fence which has a round red sign on it. Beyond turn right and keep beside the fence to pass another red sign directing you ahead over a spur of the hill. Here, there is another green post by a gate, which you go through. Turn left to walk across the top of a field to a small new wooden gate marked by a white topped post; go through and again turn left, between a fence and an ancient wall. Further on (55yds/50m) bear half right to cross the field, then descend a narrow valley, winding right and then left, to join a track.

4 Turn left towards two gates in a wall and take the left one with a red sign. Beyond, climb to a bench, conveniently situated with a wonderful view across to Ardnamurchan, Rum, Muck and Eigg. Afer a pause here, climb again behind the bench to an extensive area of old settlements, with the remains of houses, walls and byres, and a circular stone-lined depression, once a corn-drying kiln. Go across to a distinct path, which runs right, and follow it out onto the wave-cut platform on the east side of Caliach Point. Walk over the close-cropped turf, where flocks of twites feed in summer and keep a watch for whales, dolphins and porpoises. The path winds round through a gap and crosses a slope, then climbs up to a narrow col. There before you is the sea on the other side, with breakers rolling in. Gulls and kittiwakes wheel around, harried from time to time by great skuas. Turn right and walk across the narrow neck of land to the point and enjoy the panoramic view. There is a huge patch of roseroot on the cliff below.

5 Return over the grassy bridge and climb the easy slope beyond to the trig point and another fine view. Then make your way towards the western edge of the headland, but keep high, following small paths along the edge. Steeply below is the 100ft/30m platform, then cliffs to the sea. Carry on round the edge to a small gap between knolls to pick up a path, which swings right and then left to come down gently to the old settlement seen earlier. Go back to the gate with the red sign.

6 You now have three choices for the return to Calgary. If you want to go down to the road end at Calaich, go ahead on the track from the gate with the red sign, past a caravan on the left and a cottage on the right, through a gate and out onto the road. There is parking 110yds/100m along the road if you are being picked up, or you can walk the 3 miles/5km along the minor,

Great Skua

virtually traffic-free road to Calgary. It joins the B8073 about 330yds/300m before the Hotel. Turn right to return to your car. Otherwise retrace your steps along the lovely wave-cut platform, enjoying the views the other way round.

Roseroot

Practicals

Type of walk: A pleasing ramble with some spectacular coastal scenery. It is fairly dry and there are paths. The waymarks are far apart but clear.

Total Distance:	8 miles/13km whichever way you return. It could be divided into two, with the walk round Caliach Point being a separate one done from the parking area at Calaich.
Time:	4 hours
Maps:	OS Explorer 374/Landranger 47
NB:	There is a discrepancy in the spelling of the name; the OS gives Caliach for the point and also for the farm near it, but all the signs spell it Calaich.

10

Treshnish Coast Walk

Park in the quarry car park, grid ref 361485. This lies two miles south of Calgary, on the left hand side of the B8073, beyond the track to Treshnish Farm.

The remains of the carefully constructed cottages and barns of **Glac Gugairidh** and **Crackaig**, visited on this walk, make for moving viewing. What hard work went into the construction of the dwellings. Look for the rounded corners of the roofless buildings, the stone walls of the cottages still standing up to their wall heads, and the fine remnants of boundary walls. What hard work, too, it must have been to carry up the harvest of the land and the sea to the villages above. Maybe the people who lived here were on the emigrant ship that sailed from Calgary Bay, 'cleared' to provide a great sheep run for the landowner. Some records suggest that the settlements were deserted around 1860, possibly due to an epidemic.

Coast below Crackaig

Walk 10

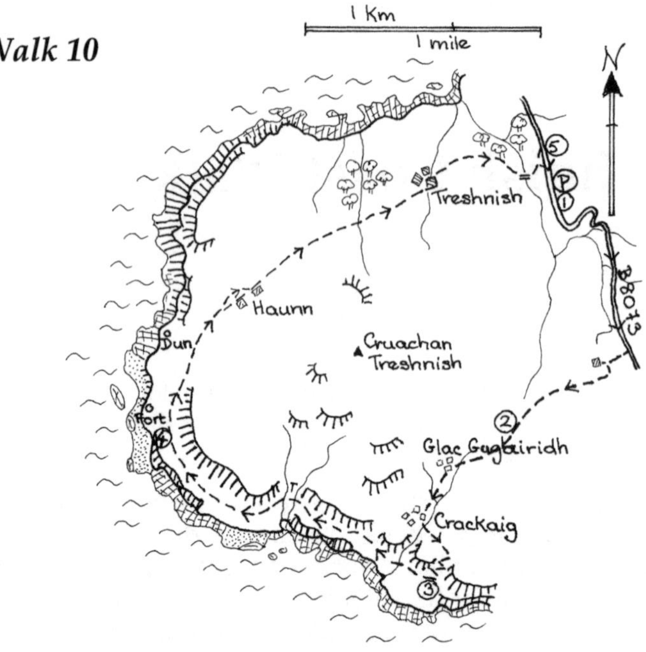

1 Turn left out of the parking area and walk with care uphill, soon to pass a small woodland from where resound, in spring, the calls of willow warblers. Carry on the narrow road for just over half a mile to turn right up an access track, signed Lariach Mhor, from where there is a fine view of the island of Coll. Just before the dwelling, the old schoolhouse, turn left to walk a signed footpath. Follow the arrows that direct you round right, and over a little stream. Continue on the path to go through the small gate, beside a farm gate. Walk on along the distinct path and where it divides take the right track. The level way continues over the moorland. Just before you reach a wide drainage ditch, leave the path, right, curve round a huge boulder and follow a little path made by earlier walkers. This leads to a narrower place to cross. Wind left to return to the good track.

2 Go on to reach the top of a little hillock from where you have a superb view of the Treshnish Isles. Over to your right is a small lochan. Scramble down some easy rocks to come parallel with an ancient wall, on your right. Then stroll a grassy swathe to reach the abandoned ruined settlement of Glac Gugairidh from where, across the sea, you can see the Abbey and sandy beaches on Iona. This is a lovely corner where you will want to pause; stonecrop grows along the old walls and wheatears flit about the stones. Continue on down the grassy swathe to reach a second ruined settlement, Crackaig, sheltered from the weather by the inland side of a huge craggy cliff. Here several ash trees provide shade. Bear left after you have explored the township, step over a stream and follow the path that leads to a wide gully, which drops steeply and for a long way, between cliffs, to the wave-cut platform below. The distinct path goes down in wide easy zigzags that make the descent very comfortable. Pause often to enjoy the views out to sea.

Wheatear

3 At the bottom, turn right and begin your walk along the raised beach, with the sea well down to the left, and with huge cliffs rearing up to your right. Follow the good path along the glorious turf. Pass through an old wall where yellow flags grow and stonechats chack. At the edge of a narrow burn, look up to see the stream descending a very steep narrow gorge – this is the little stream that flowed below Crackaig, crossed below the ash trees and then dropped down the sheer-sided gully. Avoid wet patches as you continue but generally there is a dry path close-by. Wind round two small bays and in a boggy area, to the side of the path, look for the pretty pink bog pimpernel. Stroll on with the Treshnish Isles seeming very close. Then follow the little path as it descends to a lower raised beach. Here pause, and turn half left, to see the Paps of Jura behind the Ross of Mull, and Gometra at the west end of Ulva.

4 Once past a tall crumbling sea stack, with an archway through a smaller stack at its base, follow the rising path up the cliff edge to curve round the top of an extensive bay. At the far side stands Dun Haunn. Go on up a continuing wide track, leading away from the shore, to a gate with a board that tells you it is '2.1 miles to the B-road'. Beyond, strike diagonally across a pasture and then keep to the left of the old village of Haunn, now holiday

accommodation. Continue on a narrow path through a colourful hay-meadow, which joins the access track to the cottages, where you turn left. In June look for the glorious array of orchids, which include butterfly, fragrant and northern marsh, lining the right bank of the track. As you go on enjoy the view of Rum. Pass through gates to arrive at Treshnish Farm and Cottages. Curve round left and then right to continue on the gated way. Follow the track as it begins to descend, passing another old schoolhouse, crossing the pretty Ensay Burn and continue to the road.

5 Turn right and walk on, with care, along the narrow road to the parking area in the quarry.

Bog pimpernel

Practicals

Type of walk: A superb walk over moorland, past two interesting old settlements and then along the delightful Treshnish coast. The final 2 miles are along a wide reinforced inland track.

Total Distance:	7 miles/11.4km
Time:	3–4 hours
Maps:	OS Explorer 374/Landranger 47

11

Dun Aisgain and Loch Tuath

Park opposite Kilninian church, Torloisk, grid ref 396457. This is reached from Salen or from Calgary by the B8073.

Dun Aisgain, a well preserved Iron Age hillfort, stands on the summit of a low hill, on the 100ft/30m raised beach, south-west of Burg farmhouse, Torloisk. It faced the sea as a defence against an enemy approaching from the Loch Tuath – the North Loch. It has an inner and an outer wall.

1 From the church return to the narrow road and walk east, for nearly two miles. Pass Torloisk House with its splendid turreted roof, set amid trees. Go on past the two cottages of Achleck and then Normans Ruh. Next pass two cottages on the left, followed by a ruined house on the right. Beyond, go through a gate, on the right, and follow a grassy way that swings right, round the corner of a ruin. Keep right across the pasture to a stile over the fence. Walk ahead to cross the next stile and continue to a track that goes downhill to a sturdy pier jutting into Rainich Bay.

Dun Aisgain

Walk 11

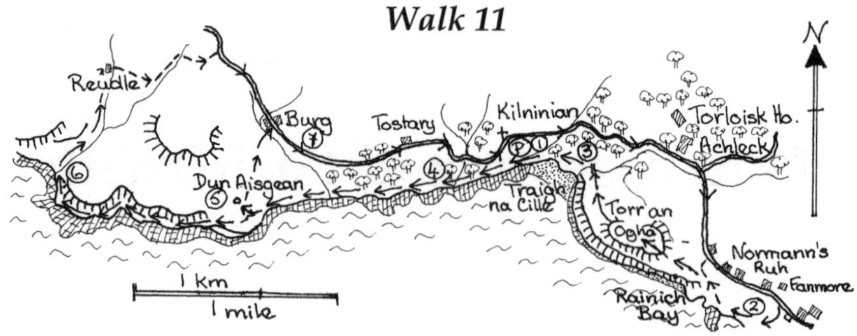

2 Ignore the way to the pier and turn right to climb the reinforced track. Where it zigzags right, strike off left along a grassy way. Follow it as it continues to climb through a rocky gully onto a hill, Torr an Ogha, which you cross. Descend through another short rocky gully and follow the path as it swings right, inland, towards a footbridge over the Allt a' Mhuilinn and a large sheep dip. Once across the footbridge, bear left. Step across a small stream and walk on to join a track coming in on your right. Follow it towards the shore and then cross another footbridge.

3 Go on above the delightful sands of Traigh na Cille. Watch out for the point where a sheep trod leads you into wind-blown birches. Step across a stream and head uphill, right, to pass through a gate in the fence. Continue along the high-level pastured way and then swing inland between grassy knolls, where you can glimpse Kilninian church. Bear left and stride on. Follow the narrow path to cross a tiny stream and pass through a gate in the fence. Walk on towards a derelict wall, with a fence beyond. Go through another gate, keeping to the path as it leads into scattered thorn and birch, close to the shore. Again, look for a narrow path that leads steadily upwards through extensive oak woodland.

4 Step across the next stream and press on. Once out of the trees, go over pasture that covers a raised beach, with stranded cliffs to your right. Negotiate another stream, taking care: the boulders can be slippery. Head seawards towards a cairn on your left from where there is a wonderful view over the loch towards the islands of Ulva and Gometra. Look west for your first sighting of Dun Aisgain and then descend to a gate in a fence. Before climbing

Eiders

upwards to explore the fortification, look at the many remains of the ruined village of Burg.

5 The dramatic galleried Iron Age fort stands on an eminence, with a commanding view of the loch. It has thick walls and several lintels. Return downhill to the ruined village and continue along a glorious stretch of raised beach. From the lovely path, look down with care on the shore far below, where eiders bask, and cormorants perch on rugged rocks. The way then swings inland as it approaches the sea outlet of the Allt Reudle.

6 Cross the Allt Reudle at a suitable crossing place and continue upwards, on the far side, to reach a white house. From here a good track leads to the road where you turn right to walk to Burg.

7 Beyond Burg stride the narrow road to pass the houses at Tostary. Begin to descend the winding road and after the first S-bend look right to see a standing stone in a pasture. Stroll on to rejoin your car close to the church.

Practicals

Type of walk: Generally easy walking along the cliffs where occasionally a head for heights is needed. Half the walk is along the narrow road, B8073, from which you obtain good views.

Total Distance:	9 miles/14.5km
Time:	5 hours
Maps:	OS Explorer 374/Landranger 48

12

Ulva Woodland Walk

Park on a flat area on the right just before you approach the Ulva ferry, grid ref 447399. There is another car park a short distance along, on the left, but the approach to it is steep and badly rutted. To reach the ferry, take the B8073 for 6 miles/ 9.5km along the north side of Loch na Keal. The left turn for the ferry is well signposted.

The **ferry** runs from 9am to 5pm, Mondays to Fridays, on demand. There is NO ferry on Saturdays. Ulva is open for visitors on Sundays from June 1 to the end of August. The ferry is for foot passengers only but it will carry bicycles. Camping is strictly by permission. Dogs must be kept on the lead at all times. During lambing time, April 1 until May 31, dogs are restricted to certain areas. Walking boots and waterproofs are recommended. Enquiries Ulva ferry 01688 500226. Boathouse/Visitor Centre/ Restaurant 01688 500241 – why not book a meal to be ready for you on your return from your walk?

Sheila's Cottage, Ulva

Walk 12

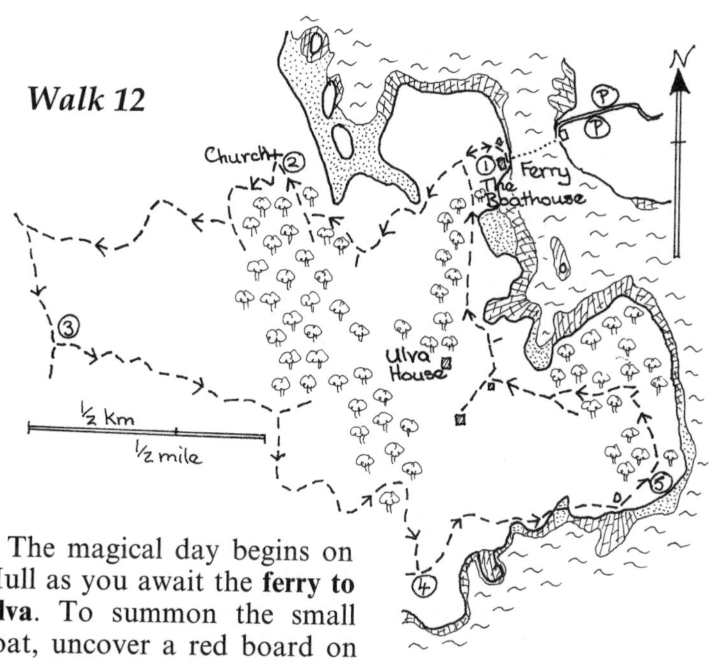

The magical day begins on Mull as you await the **ferry to Ulva**. To summon the small boat, uncover a red board on the side of a building on the tiny jetty. The ferryman, who comes across when signalled, asks that visitors close the cover over the red board, after use, so that he doesn't have to make any unnecessary trips. The ferry takes two minutes to cross the Sound of Ulva. You pay for the trip at Ulva's tearoom, 'The Boathouse', by the jetty. Then you start your walk on the island where time seems to stand still – at least for visitors.

There are no tarmac roads on the island. In the early 19th century 600 inhabitants lived in 16 townships, maintained by a thriving but labour-intensive **kelp industry**. All who could work did so on the seashore cutting, carrying and burning the seaweed. Then when the bottom fell out of the kelp market the crofts, already neglected, were struck by potato blight. This resulted in the crofting population having no jobs or food. By 1851 only 150 people remained. The crofters had gone to North America or Australia, their passages paid for by the Highlands and Islands Emigration Society and ⅓ contribution from the landowner.

1 Follow the signpost for 'All Routes' outside The Boathouse, walking right and passing the restored Sheila's Cottage, on your right. At the next signpost go ahead, soon to pass a track going off right, which you ignore. Remain on the winding main track, lined with lush vegetation. Bear right at the next junction and continue uphill until you reach a T-junction of tracks. Here take the right turn, signposted to the church. Just before you reach it you pass the old manse, where you might spot siskins, greenfinches and a woodpecker. Go through the open door into the vast high-ceilinged church. The main part is used as the village hall and a smaller section, separated by folding doors, is for worship. It was designed by Thomas Telford and built in 1827–28. Occasional services are held in the church and Christenings and weddings. There is an amazing high pulpit with a canopy.

2 Return to the gate of the church and walk up a narrow track, now on your right, signed 'Woodland Walk', to pass through deciduous trees and walled by natural rock. Eventually the path emerges from the trees and becomes a fine grassy path, through bracken. Follow it as it drops down and winds left. At the bottom of the slope a signpost with 'Minister's Road, a short-cut to the main track', written on it, directs you right through a gate onto the open fell. Look right across Loch Tuath to see the magnificent Eas Fors waterfall on the mainland of Mull. Follow the good, relatively high-level path, and then go with it as it descends into a little valley before climbing again. Continue on the pleasing way to join the main track to Gometra at a sturdily built sheepfold, where you turn left and walk on.

3 At the next signpost, turn left, remaining on the main track. As you descend and reach another post, signed 'Wood and Shore walk', turn right and take the little green path across a tiny burn and walk up through birch. Enjoy this delightful path and follow it as it leads out into a clearing with a field of wavy grass on the right. The path moves through more woodland and then on through bracken, from where there are magnificent views of the Mull mainland. Carry on down the path, following the white-topped low posts. Wind across a boggy area before reaching the next post. As you descend, look right to see the Clark memorial standing high on a conical

Whitethroat

hill, the site of an old fort, Dun Bhioramuill. Follow the waymarked path as it passes through trees, the haunt of a tawny owl, and on over duckboarding to arrive at a deer fence, where you turn right and go down through scattered birch to arrive at a signpost, held in place by a piece of farm machinery.

4 Turn left to follow the 'Shore walk'. Here you might wish to move off the path for a few steps to look down on a curving bay where otters have been spotted, although you might see them all along this shore. Pass through a gate to arc round the next bay and follow the signpost directing you to the shore, which is littered with boulders. Cross a little stretch of salt marsh, stepping from grassy tuft to grassy tuft. Look ahead to see the next waymark that sends you on to cross a small storm beach. Head on to an obvious ladderstile over a wall. Follow the path up the slope, through the bracken, and wind round sharply right to pass a white painted stone.

5 Curve on round right, along the top of the cliff to climb some pleasingly constructed steps to a higher level. Turn right and then left, to walk on through buttercup and clover meadows, the way flanked with white stones. Go through a gate at the end of the path and wind round right and follow the path as it curves left again. It crosses a small footbridge and continues through ancient woodland, to a large rock marked in white. The path moves into a planting of oaks. Pass through a gap in the wall and continue with the wall beside you. Curve round and down and out into a pasture with a wall on your left. Go through a gate. Cut across the corner of a buttercup meadow to join a track. Turn right and at the signpost follow the direction for the ferry. At a T-junction wind right to go through a gate and at the next T-junction turn right to descend to the ferry.

Practicals

Type of walk: This is a wonderful walk, unobtrusively signposted, with good paths and tracks.

Total Distance: 5 miles/8km
Time: 3–4 hours
Maps: OS Explorer 375/Landranger 48

13

Ulva; basalt columns and old villages

For details on reaching the island see previous walk (walk 12).

General Lachlan MacQuarrie was the most famous member of the clan that possessed Ulva for centuries. It is believed that he was born at Ormaig. After a career in the army he became the first Governor of New South Wales and many Australians visit his mausoleum at Gruline on Mull. The mausoleum belongs to the National Trust of Australia but is maintained for them by the National Trust for Scotland. In 1773 he entertained Dr Johnson and James Boswell. In 1777 Lachlan had to sell Ulva to pay his debts. Look for MacQuarrie gravestones in the burial ground at Kilvekewan.

Volcanic activity near the present day Ben More, on Mull, poured forth layers of molten lava. As this cooled **basalt columns** formed. Many millennia later glacial action exposed them and

Basalt cliffs, Ulva

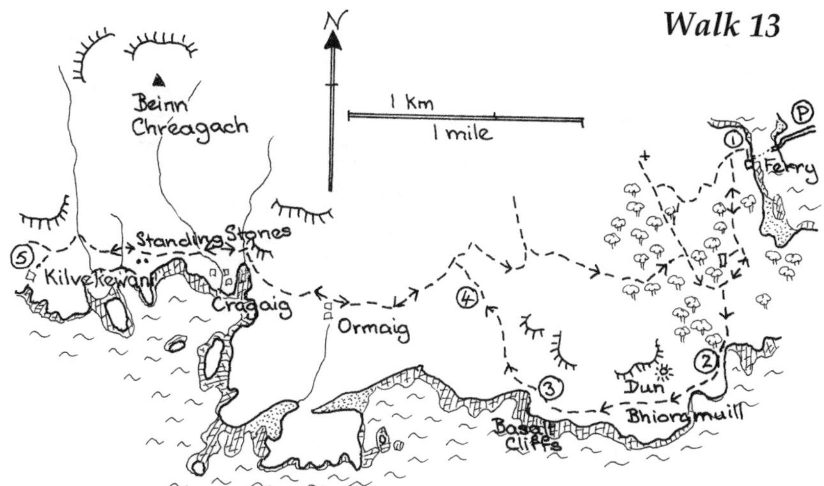

the terraced landscape you see so clearly on the south side of Ulva. Raised beaches, wave-cut platforms and sea caves high up on hillsides far from the sea are the result of changing sea levels.

Over 200 years ago the father and grandfather of the missionary and explorer David Livingstone lived in **Livingstone's Cave** while waiting for a croft house to be built. Archeologists studying the floor found that they weren't the first occupants. Shells, flint artefacts and fragments of bone were found dating back to around 5650 BC.

1 Leave the Boathouse and tearoom and follow the signpost for 'All routes'. Keep left of Sheila's Cottage and walk the track. At the first signpost, turn left for the 'basalt rocks' and carry on along the track to pass beside the glorious deciduous woodland of Ulva House. The latter was built in the 1950s on the site of a large early 19th century house destroyed by fire. Ignore the turning for the 'woodland walk' and go ahead through a gate and continue towards Bracadale farm. Just before the outbuildings, follow the signpost to walk left along a walled track and out onto open pasture towards the sea. Bear right and press on through the next gate, which brings you out onto a small headland, with a grand view across Loch na Keal. Here you might spot otters.

2 Walk ahead to follow another signpost for the 'basalt rocks'; the post has a piece of farm machinery at its base. Go on along the

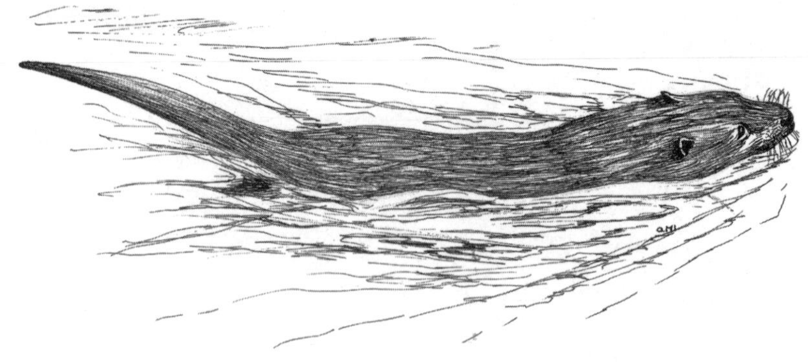

Otter

little path to pass through a broken wall into woodland. Cross a burn and continue uphill to where the path forks. If you wish to see the burial ground of the Clark family on Dun Bhioramuill, take the right branch and follow it uphill. The huge marble monuments lie inside a high gateless wall. Visiting the memorial involves a difficult pathless scramble. Otherwise take the left branch and continue along a promontory. The path then curves down to the edge of the wood, climbs a little, goes down again and soon comes out of the trees onto a wave-cut platform. Walk over the turf to the edge to view the superb columns.

3 Carry on along the little path on the edge of the cliffs and follow it inland, past traces of lazy-beds where potatoes were grown in raised areas on soil taken from either side. To the right of the path, up a slope, tucked into the base of a high basalt-stranded cliff, is Livingstone's Cave. Go on along the path to a large grassy area around which are scattered the ruins of several houses. Cross a stream and climb the slope to see a house similar to the one the Livingstone family lived in, with a dramatic view from the doorway.

4 Continue on the sloping way, through birch woodland, to join and follow a track that continues to climb as it swings left. Stride on enjoying the magnificent views out to sea and then follow the track as it begins to descend towards the ruined village of Ormaig. Stroll on along the way to the head of a small muddy tidal inlet to see an old cruck mill. Two large millstones lie on the grassy floor. Walk on along the way, which brings you to the ruined village of Cragaig, where even more houses crowd the lovely slopes of the sheltering cliffs. As you pass two standing stones, away to your left, look out to sea towards several small islands, where many seals bask. Then continue to the ruined village of Kilvekewan. Drop down the slopes, seaward, to visit the ruined graveyard, where several MacQuarries are buried.

5 Return along the track to where you joined it above the birch wood. Carry on along the track to reach the main track, where you turn right and follow the well signposted way back to the ferry, with perhaps enough time left to enjoy the excellent refreshments at the tearoom, before taking the last ferry to Mull.

Birch

Practicals

Type of walk: This is another delightful walk on a lovely island. Good paths and tracks and just a little climbing will be enjoyed by all.

Total Distance:	10 miles/16km. With the excellent way-marking you can return to ferry if the walk seems too long.
Time:	5–6 hours
Maps:	OS Explorer 375/Landranger 48. There is a helpful map in the Visitor's Guide, purchased at the Tearoom.

14

Loch Ba

Park in a small parking area, grid ref 545388. This is reached by taking the B8035 from Salen and continuing on past the right turn for Killechronan. Pass the left turns for MacQuarrie family mausoleum and the Gruline Estate to carry on to cross a fine old bridge, over the River Ba, built at the time of the Clearances. Just beyond is the parking area at Knock farm, which lies at the corner where the B-road makes a sharp right turn.

Loch Ba is a beautiful sheet of water, two miles in length, and almost completely surrounded by high hills, some of which are clad in woodland on their lower slopes. At the foot of the loch nestles Gruline House, sited on vast amounts of glacial material,

Loch Ba

which separates Loch Ba from Loch na Keal. The hills at the head of the loch were formed during the Tertiary volcanic period and are the remains of at least three collapsed volcanoes. The geology here is very complex and much studied.

1 Take the right of way that goes ahead from the right, or south, of the parking area, along a track through deciduous woodland. Ignore a track that soon climbs right and go on to walk beside the loch. At first deciduous trees climb the steep slopes to the right and through these flit many small birds. Along the shore, in spring and summer, sandpipers rear their broods and close-by oyster catchers tend their young. On the water mergansers fish and above you might spot a sea eagle, believed to nest in trees overlooking the loch. Closer to the track lie many rocks and boulders, erratics left by the receding glacier.

2 The rather unsympathetically reinforced track (at the time of writing) continues along beside the shoreline, passing through small groups of deciduous trees until, after two miles, you reach a Y-junction. Ignore the right branch (newly reinforced), which ascends steadily up Glen Clachaig. This is an old drove road that climbs over the shoulder of Ben More and then down to Glen More, once a much used short cut through the hills and today used by strong walkers.

3 Continue ahead along the shore to stand on the bridge over the River Clachaig to enjoy the view down the loch and

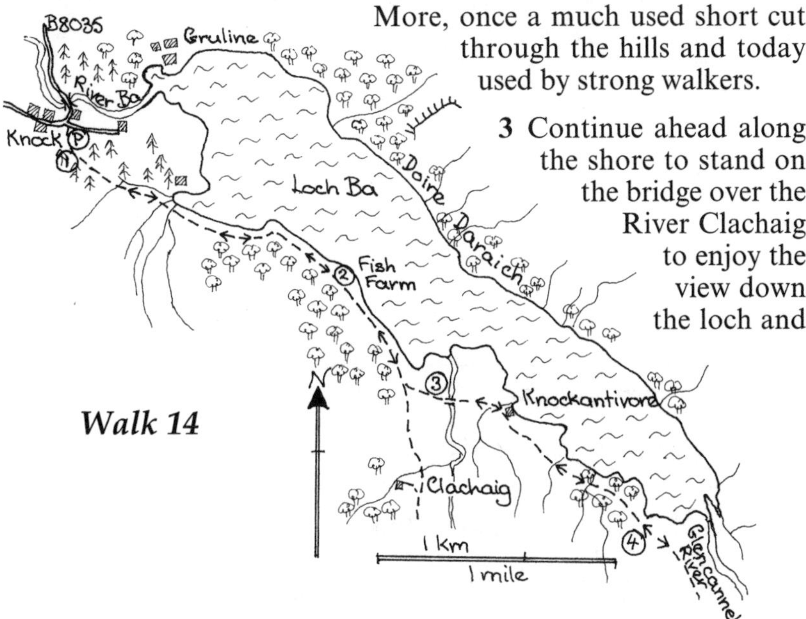

Walk 14

the mountains all around. Some walkers will wish to continue past Knockantivore, which has been restored, to the head of the loch, through another delightful birch woodland.

4 Return by the same route. The opposite shore of the loch is private and mostly pathless, with no access for walkers.

Merganser

Practicals

Type of walk: A delightful there-and-back walk, with much to see.

Total Distance: 4–5 miles/6.5–8km
Time: 2–3 hours
Maps: OS Explorer 374/Landranger 48

15

Beinn nan Gabhar and Beinn Fhada

Park in a space before (north-east) the bridge over the Scarisdale River, grid ref 517376, where there is space for 3 or 4 cars. To access this, take the B8035 from Salen, and after 3 miles keep left

Waterfall, Beinn nan Gabhar

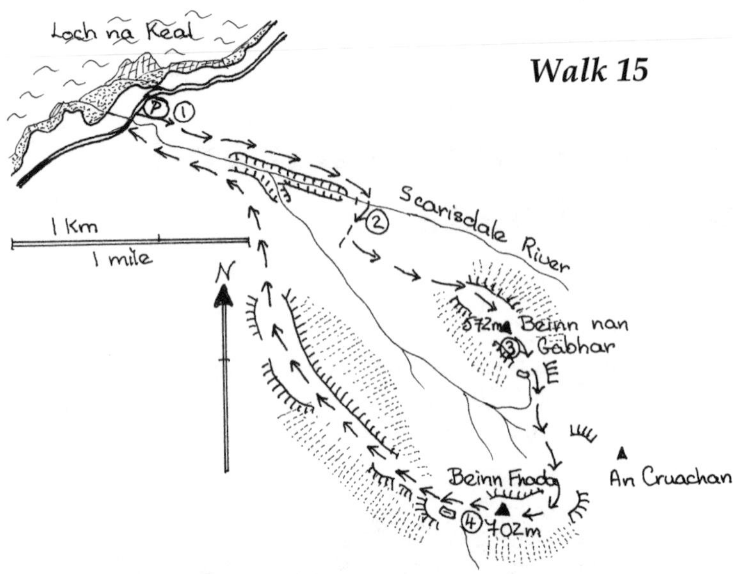

Walk 15

at the junction. Continue along the south-east shore of Loch na Keal to the bridge over the river.

Beinn Fhada (the long mountain) is 2300ft/702m high and has a fine narrow rocky ridge giving splendid views of Ben More and A'Chioch. **Beinn nan Gabhar** (mountain of goats) is considerably lower at 1845ft/572m and is tucked away out of sight from the main road, except for a short distance near the bridge, but is a worth while climb in its own right. Together they make a splendid round, which has the advantage of often being out of the cloud when Ben More to the west is wreathed in mist. They are both part of the volcanic complex which formed Mull's more spectacular mountains.

1 From the parking space, walk uphill with the Scarisdale River to your right, making use of a faint path. Go through a gate space in the wall and join a fairly boggy quad track. Follow it to the crest of a small intermediate hill where it turns south and runs along above the river. Then the track fades, but a series of sheep tracks continues just above the river, which now runs in a gorge. Keep to the lower obvious sheep path to go by a superb water chute on the river. Just above this the path goes down through a gap in the rock and crosses the river easily on natural stepping stones.

2 Continue on a path across the north end of Beinn nan Gabhar, then head up its northern ridge. Zigzag up the slope between small rock bands, often on scree, but with little difficulty, to reach the summit plateau. Walk along to the second cairn, which is the highest point.

3 Then make your way south-west from the summit, down easy grass slopes to the rounded, boggy bealach with Beinn Fhada to your right. Climb steeply to the ridge of Beinn Fhada and bear right to walk up the delightful rocky crest. The views from the top are splendid, especially across to A'Chioch and Ben More. Look for mountain hares here, quite rich brown in summer.

4 From the summit, walk north-west along the ridge for a short distance before finding your way down and left through a rocky band towards the northern end of a small lochan. From here, carry on along the ridge crest, until you come to a short rocky step. The easiest way down this is a little to the right of the crest. Once down, follow a series of animal tracks and traces of paths on along the ridge, and up over a small subsidiary summit. Descend from this, gently at first, then it becomes steeper and more awkward, with a series of rock bands. Choose your route

Mountain hare

through this steep section with care, keeping close to the ridge crest. As you approach the Scarisdale river the gradient eases. Bear left to walk above the river, heading for the shore of Loch na Keal. The route terminates in an area of bracken and peat bog, fortunately not far from the road. Make your way across this using a series of quad tracks and animal paths, coming out on the road beside the bridge. Cross it and return to your car.

Alpine Lady's Mantle

Practicals

Type of walk: This is an interesting climb of two of Mull's less frequented hills. There are no definite paths except on the ridges, but there are plenty of quad bike tracks and sheep paths to help you over the rough ground. Some care needs to be taken with route finding on Beinn Fhada, especially on the steep slope coming down, but there is no real difficulty. The ridges are quite narrow and exhilarating but are easy. All the usual safety precautions should be taken. Do not attempt in the mist.

Total Distance: 6 miles/9.5km
Time: 5–6 hours
Map: OS Explorer 375/Landranger 48

16

Ben More

Park beside the road along the south side of Loch na Keal by the bridge over the Abhainn na h-Uamha, grid ref 507368. There is room on the grass on either side of the bridge on the inland side. Do not park on the shore side. You can also park on the grass on the shore side of the road, opposite the track to Dhiseig farm, grid ref 494359. To access these parking areas, leave Salen by the B8035. After 3 miles take the left branch at the road junction to continue along the south-east shore of Loch na Keal.

Ben More, at 3015ft/966m, is the **highest mountain on Mull**, the only island Munro outside Skye. It is also the only basalt Munro.

Ben More from A'Choich

Walk 16

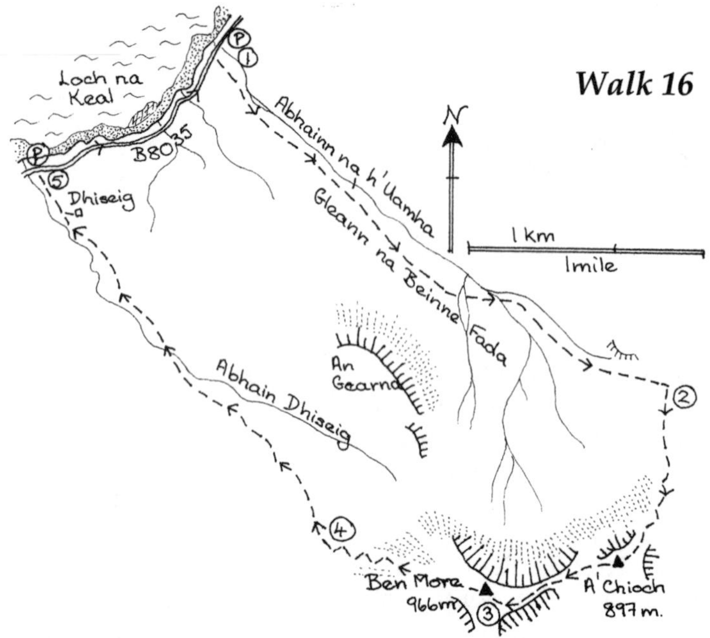

It has a fine shape, with its summit at the apex of three ridges of which the ridge from A'Chioch is the most dramatic. It dominates the other mountains in the south-west of Mull and provides splendid views from Loch na Keal to the north and from the Ross to the south. Because of its height and position at the seaward end of the range it collects cloud, and frequently is the only mountain wreathed in mist on an otherwise glorious day. Choose your weather carefully, and be prepared for it to change. Ben More is a huge mountain and any ascent must be taken seriously.

1 Walk up the path on the south-west side of the Abhainn na h-Uamha. If parked at Dhiseig walk along the lovely turf behind the shore for 1 mile/1.5km to this point. The path heads up by the sparkling burn, which is full of pools, rapids and waterfalls. At one point you are walking along level with the tops of trees in the gorge. Take care on the path because it is very wet in places and you will need to find ways round the worst bogs. Climb up beside a band of dark rock where the burn descends in a fine waterfall, and gain the upper corrie, where it is not quite so wet. Cross the burn, easy in normal weather, and walk a gravel path up the

ridge beyond. This gradually becomes less distinct; if in doubt head left to the crest of the spur and find a quad bike track which you follow all the way to the bealach. Pause to admire the view of all Mull's southern mountains.

Ravens

2 Then turn right and climb the narrowing ridge to A'Chioch. It looks daunting but is nowhere near as hard as it looks. The path winds across the ridge backwards and forwards, with rocky staircases to scramble up at frequent intervals. The only real difficulty is the exposure; this is not a route for anyone without a head for heights. Soon the ridge broadens and you reach the top of A'Chioch. The ridge ahead, linking A'Chioch to Ben More, looks even worse but in fact is quite straightforward. Go down easily to the col below. Then follow a small path, which winds its way along the south side of the ridge. The top of the ridge forms a wall beside you all the way across, and because of this the sense of exposure is greatly reduced. There are occasional gaps giving a fine view to the north. Take higher paths where you have a choice, to avoid getting into scree lower down. The hardest bit is the steep scramble up to the summit of Ben More at the end. Many little paths go up, all with rock steps and some scree; avoid getting too far to the left and zigzag up, choosing the way which seems easiest.

3 The slope then eases and suddenly you are on the summit, right beside the cairn, a circular wall inside which you can shelter from the wind. The view is splendid, from Jura in the south, Coll and Tiree and maybe the Outer Hebrides to the west and Rum and Eigg to the north. To the east are all the mainland hills; too many to name, although you can have fun trying to work them out. Ravens circle round the summit, probably hoping to scavenge the remains of packed lunches. The way off the top is obvious, a wide clear path running north-west along the level summit ridge, with fine cliffs to the right edging the corrie below. Follow the path on down through the scree which clothes the top of the hill; the path zigzags to give an easy descent. At frequent intervals it is marked with cairns.

4 Lower down it becomes less steep and grassier. The Abhainn Dhiseig on the right has waterfalls and pools and eventually the path comes down to ford it, then carries on along the bank through a delightful grassy, flowery valley. It keeps beside the burn until you reach a fence. Walk right for about 55yds/50m, go through a gate and come back along the other side, or just step over the fence as everyone else does, to carry on above the burn, now in a shallow gorge. At the next fence go through the gate and come down to a farm track past a fine metal sign saying 'UP' and an arrow pointing back the way you have come. Turn left and follow the track down to the shore. There is a notice saying 'This track is the way up Ben More. Park on the shore, keep dogs on leads, and in the shooting season mid-August to October 20 contact Benmore Estate on 01680 300229.'

5 Return to your car if it is here, or walk the mile along the grass above the shore to the other parking area.

Practicals

Type of walk: The ridge from A'Chioch is splendid and a very fine way to climb the mountain. It is not particularly difficult but it is exposed. If you have no head for heights or don't enjoy scrambling then you should go up by the route of descent from Dhiseig and back down the same way. This is very straight forward and it would be quite hard to get lost even in mist (of which there is a lot).

Total Distance: 7 miles/11.2km
Time: 5–6 hours
Maps: OS Explorer 375/Landranger 48

17

MacKinnon's Cave

Use the car park provided about 110yds/100m before the farm, on the right of the track, grid ref 448333. There is a board

MacKinnon's Cave

showing the route to the cave and a warning about the tide. Access to the car park is by the B8035, which runs along the south shore of Loch na Keal. Just before the road begins to climb the steep slopes over the Ardmeanach peninsula, take a small road on the right to Balmeanach Farm.

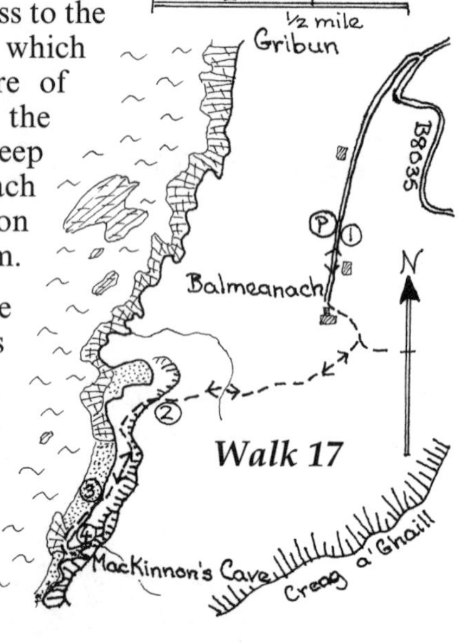

The cave is said to be the deepest in the Hebrides. It is blocked by a rockfall at its inner end. It gets its name from the **Abbot MacKinnon**, who lived in it for a while. Apparently he moved there from a cave on Staffa, where he found the sea made so much noise it interrupted his meditations.

There is a **legend** associated with this cave. In an attempt to find how big the cave was, a group of men, lightly armed and accompanied by a piper and a dog, went in to explore. A second group went over the top, listening for the sound of the pipes to trace their progress. The second group heard the tune change to a call for help, then the piper seemed to turn back and the music stopped suddenly. They rushed down to help, but found the

Rock doves

bodies of the first group hacked to pieces, with the piper nearest the mouth of the cave. The dog apparently turned up later at Tavool on the other side of the headland – completely hairless.

Boswell and Johnson visited the cave on their tour of the Hebrides and, undeterred by the legend, measured the cave, using a walking stick and with only a candle to give them light.

Purple loosestrife

1 Walk on, following the direction indicated by an arrow, to pass the house on your left. Go through a gate into the farmyard and bear left on a good track to wind round a barn and through another gate. Both gates have notices on asking you to close them. Flocks of twites feed on grass seeds here in summer. Take the track up by the fence, and where it turns away left go right and follow the fence towards the coast. There are arrows on the fence at intervals and a sign 'Cave' at one point. Cut across a corner in the fence on pleasant short turf to go through a small gate. A sign beside it says 'to MacKinnon's Cave' and again warns you to watch the tide.

2 Go ahead down a small valley, which comes to the edge of the cliff. There is a superb view along the cliffs of the Ardmeanach peninsula, with Iona visible at the end. Keep left and wind round under an outcrop; go down a sloping slab of rock and then descend an easy path to the shore. Agrimony, meadowsweet and marsh woundwort grow in profusion under the cliff. Cross the pebbles at the top of the beach, then go along a small path through a reedbed with meadowsweet and purple loosestrife. Then walk over more pebbles. Look for flights of rock doves along the cliffs; many nest here in the caves.

3 The way goes through or over great boulders on the beach, which is time-consuming, and over a ridged sloping spur of rock, which

is very easy to cross. Go round the corner and assuming the tide is low enough, into the cave. There is a fall of water droplets across the opening. If you have a torch you can explore the enormous cave; it does feel rather eerie and in certain wind conditions you can hear a whistling which adds to the strangeness.

4 Return before the tide comes in.

Primroses

Practicals

Type of walk: Short and well-signed, mostly over easy ground. Keep dogs on a lead over farm ground. The boulders on the beach can be awkward unless you are very confident, but the distance is short. Try to approach the cave on an ebb tide so that you have plenty of time; it is only accessible from about half tide (depending on wind and weather) and if you were to be cut off it would be a long wait. If you wish to explore the cave take a good torch.

Total Distance:	2 miles/3.4km
Time:	1½–2 hours
Maps:	OS Explorer 375/Landranger 48
NB:	Tide tables are available from local shops, or from the Internet (www.ukho.gov.uk). Select EasyTide and click on Iona; this will give you the tide times (in GMT) for the next week.

18

Burg and the Fossil Tree

Park at grid ref 478276. To reach this drive past Tiroran House, through a gate (at which point the road becomes a track), and on for 330yds/300m to a car park.

The Fossil Tree

Walk 18

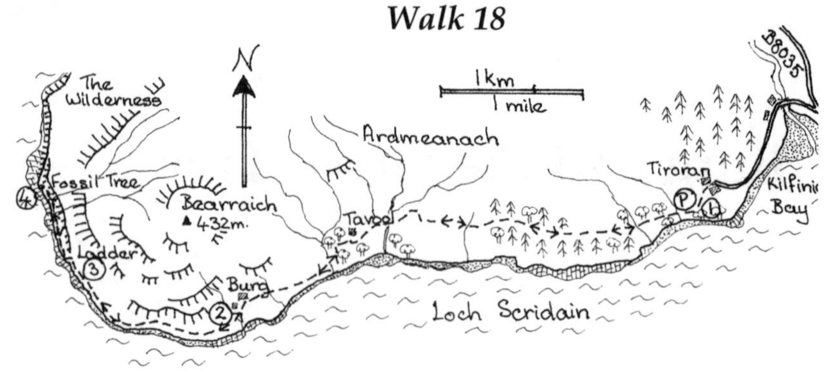

To access this, turn west off the B8035 where it leaves the shore of Loch Scridain to go up Glen Seilisdeir and cross the hill. The minor road is signed to Tiroran, and there is a National Trust for Scotland sign to Burg and the fossil tree.

The Fossil Tree was found by John MacCulloch in 1819. It is about 5ft/1.6m across and was evidently sufficiently large to cool the lava which overwhelmed it, so that it was preserved. It is 50 million years old; at the time of its discovery the impression in the cliff was still lined with 2ins/4cm of charcoal. Most of this has now gone, collected by souvenir hunters, so all that is left is the huge groove with a small section of trunk at the base now capped with cement to try to preserve it. The joints in the basalt round the tree have been distorted because of its cooling influence; it is thought that there were other trees there, too, which contributed to the general cooling effect.

Basalt lava often has bubbles of gas in it, which form cavities when the lava has solidified. Later these may fill up with solutions of silica which percolate through the rock; the silica may form quartz crystals on the walls of the cavities, or it may solidify in concentric bands to form translucent agates. These are harder than the basalt so they weather out and can be found as pebbles on the beach.

The unusual basalt formations on the shore may also be the result of cooling due to trees.

1 Walk on along the track from the car park. After a short distance, 330yds/300m, take the right fork at a Y-junction. Carry on along the easy level way for 2½ miles/4km. Look for the remains of old settlements on either side of the track, although these may be hard to see when the bracken is high. Cross a burn below a fine waterfall and continue to Tavool. The track divides before Tavool House; take the left branch signed 'Fossil tree', which goes through a gateway and continues on through a wood, crossing two attractive streams. Beyond the wood the track continues to Burg farm, where it divides again. Take the lower, left, fork, which takes you round to the left of the farm buildings and across to a small bothy. The track stops here, and a path continues beyond.

2 A short distance beyond the bothy, the path passes a monument to the memory of Daisy Cheape, who drowned near here in a boating accident. The monument stands on a hillock to the left, and there is a series of small cliffs on the right. The path then turns northwards along the slope above the shore, and begins to descend at a shallow angle, coming down to the shoreline after 110yds/100m or so. The flowers are abundant; look for grass of Parnassus, thyme, centaury and field felwort. After a while, the path ascends again to avoid a steeper rocky section, passing below a series of cliffs (effectively it runs along the top of one lava flow, where the flow above has been eroded to form a terrace along the hillside). Look down from here towards the beach, to see some fine examples of cooling joints within the basalt flows, including curves, a fan and a wheel shape. However it is a difficult scramble down to the shore and impossible at high tide, when the sea comes well up the cliff, so just admire them from above. Watch out for wild goats anywhere along here, and you might see a peregrine fly over. Ravens and buzzards are common.

Peregrine

3 Continue on the path between several large boulders before abruptly descending a short way to an iron ladder. This ladder is not in the best of health, and whilst it was all right when the walk was being researched, it should be treated with care. Perhaps only one person should be on it at any time. Those of a more nervous disposition may prefer not to descend. From the bottom of the ladder, drop down the last few yards/metres to the beach along an easy path. Walk on along the shingle, picking your way between boulders. Look for agate pebbles, which form in holes in the basalt and then weather out. Pass two splendid waterfalls coming over the cliffs, and carry on round a corner in the cliff face to reach the tree (this may well be awkward at high tide). The tree is spectacular, though more because of the contortions its presence seems to have caused within the cooling joints than anything else. It appears as a long groove up the cliff face.

Centaury

4 Return the way you came as it is not wise to continue round the coast; the next headland is impassable except at the lowest of tides, and the way over the top is extremely steep, rough and difficult, leading into the area known as The Wilderness.

Practicals

Type of walk: A long walk but the going is easy for most of the way. There is a good track as far as Burg and then a clear path; it is only the last section with the ladder, which some walkers may find difficult. Even if you do not want to attempt this it is worth walking out beyond Burg for the splendid views.

Total Distance: 12 miles/19km
Time: 6 hours
Maps: OS Explorer 375/Landranger 48

19

Ardtun and the Leaf Fossil Beds

Park on a convenient verge beyond Lower Ardtun, grid ref 383229, making sure not to block access. This is reached by leaving Bunessan, which is on the A849, 5 miles/8km before (east of) Fionnphort, by a narrow road signposted Ardtun. Park quite close to the first left turn.

The **fossil-leaf beds**, first recorded in the 19th century, are believed to have contained an enormous quantity of leaves and petals that dropped from trees, mainly conifers, throughout untold years, settling in layers on the muddy bottom of a shallow lake. Here they remained, undisturbed, thin layers in mudstone sandwiched between basalt. Sadly there are no fossils left, all scooped out by fossil hunters.

1 Stride the left turn to walk above Traigh Mhor which, at low tide, is a mass of seaweed-covered black

Ardmeanach from Ardtun

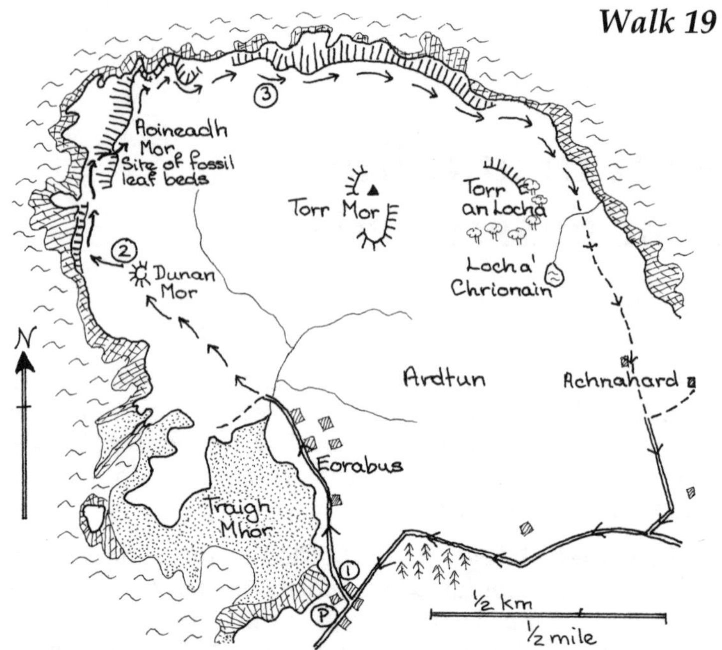

boulders. Just before the last two cottages, where the road swings left, walk ahead through a gate into pasture, which soon becomes moorland. Once over the brow, Dunan Mor lies ahead, a flat-topped hillock surmounted by a cairn. Follow the clear path, keeping to the right of the fence to reach the small hill. As you continue, follow sheep-trods around a marshy area and go on. Ahead, guarding the entrance to Loch na Lathaich stands a 'light' on a large grey rock.

2 Follow sheep trods downhill to an extensive grassy area, where lie the ruins of several houses. Walk to the edge of the low cliffs for a wonderful view of the columnar basalt, which here lies vertically, horizontally and also forms rosette patterns. Beyond the ruined houses and the magnificent basalt, rears Aoineadh Mor, a great rocky headland. Do not continue to the headland but carry on until your way is cut by a dry, rock-strewn gully in the shallow cliffs. This is where you would have once been able to see the fossil-leaf beds. Walk on to continue around the cliffs, keeping to sheep trods, through heather, avoiding as much of the wet moorland as possible. As you go look across Loch Scridain

Twites

to see the magnificent Ardmeanach headland, perhaps Mull's wildest scenery.

3 Step across a fence and continue. Do not be tempted to cut across the often wet moorland to the side of Torr na Locha but continue around the heather-edged headland to a gap in a wall. Cross the top of a grassy gully running down to a small beach. Follow animal tracks to pass through a gate in the next wall. Press on, keeping to the right side of the continuing derelict wall. Away to your right you can see Loch a' Chrionain. The way continues along a gated track, which passes between willow, rowan and honeysuckle. Pass a ruined cottage and stride on through woodland. Then the way becomes tarmacked. At the T-junction, turn right and stroll on to rejoin your car.

Practicals

Type of walk: An interesting walk with spectacular views. There are paths, tracks, and some pathless sections. Expect boggy patches after rain.

Total Distance: 4 miles/6.5km
Time: 2–3 hours
Maps: OS Explorer 373/Landranger 48

20

Tireragan Nature Reserve and Traigh Gheal

Park at grid ref 315203. To access this take the minor road, signed Knockvologan, south from Fionnphort at the west-end of the Ross. Three miles along the road go past a house on the right, with a green barn to the left. Farther on, 55yds/50m, is an area of hardcore to the left of the road with a small sign 'Walks Parking'.

Tireragan estate has been managed since 1994 by a local charity, Highland Renewal, with the intention of conserving its woodlands and encouraging their regeneration; and also

Ancient Oak, Tireragan

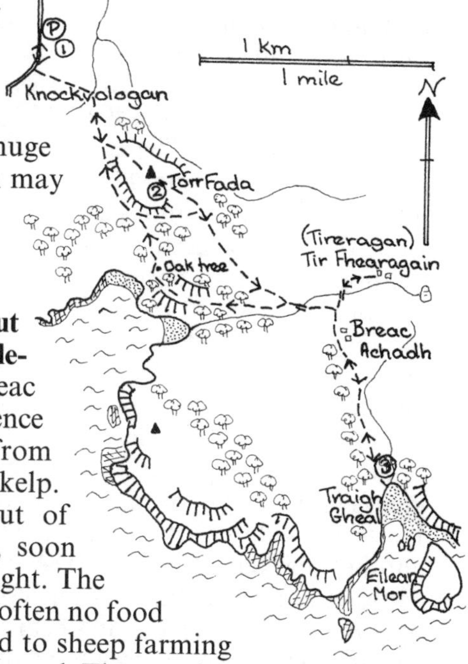

encouraging public access and enjoyment of the area. The woods are mainly of birch and hazel but there is a lot of sessile oak, bent by the winds off the Atlantic, including one huge but horizontal tree which may be the oldest oak on Mull. Deer and sheep are excluded to allow regrowth.

In the early **1800s about 100 people lived in the settlements** of Tireragan and Breac Achadh, living on subsistence farming and the income from collecting and burning kelp. Then the bottom fell out of the market for kelp ash, soon followed by the potato blight. The people had no money and often no food and the landowners looked to sheep farming to make money for them instead. The people were removed from the land, often brutally. By 1861 there was no one left living at Tireragan, only the roofless houses which you see today.

1 Walk on along the road to pass a cottage on the left, then turn left to pass between two farm buildings and go through a gate. There is a box attached to the fence containing leaflets giving details of the Nature Reserve. Head on along a stony path, which soon becomes grassy. Go through a deer gate, cross a bridge over a ditch and bear right along a well-made path. Cross the next bridge and go through another deer gate, the entrance to the nature reserve. Shortly after the entrance there is a granite boulder in the path with two arrows carved into it. Follow the left one of these. The path goes uphill through a short stretch of bracken and then onto open moorland to the top of Torr Fada. The views from this small summit are excellent, to Ardmeanach with Ben More behind and then the other south Mull mountains. To the west is Iona with Erraid in front, and to the south scattered islets and Dubh Artach lighthouse in the distance.

2 Follow the path as it descends quite steeply through bracken and birch, then crosses open ground to join another path. Turn left and continue up the valley and across an area of high moorland, then down to another valley. There is another carved stone here; follow the arrow pointing left along the obvious path. Cross the bog on a good path to a burn and turn left to go along the bank to a bridge. Cross and continue along the bank on the far side. The bog is full of meadowsweet, valerian and brilliant spikes of purple loosestrife in summer; in spring there are great clumps of yellow iris, and marsh cinquefoil lines the path. Listen for sedge warblers rattling in the bushes. In a clearing is another marked stone; take the left turn which takes you back across the burn and uphill for a short distance beside a deer fence to come to the ruins of Tir Fhearagain, from which the reserve gets its name. Two houses have quite substantial remains, one with a chimney. Return along the path to the stone and turn left. There are wet patches on the path where it goes through willow thickets, but usually there are ways round. Go past the ruins of another village, Breac Achadh, and then cross another high boggy area. There are planks across the runnels but some of these are in a state of disrepair; however usually it doesn't matter and there is a way round. The path runs along the right side of the bog, keeping to higher ground, until it begins the descent to Traigh Gheal. Here scrub has encroached on the path, making it quite difficult to proceed in places; although the path is good underfoot you have to push your way through the small trees and bracken. Cross a bog at the bottom and come out onto the most beautiful beach. It is a silver white sand beach with an island, Eilean Mor, sheltering it from the south. Although you can see the Paps of Jura as you come down the path, from the beach they are hidden behind the island; but the end of Colonsay is visible with Islay behind. Common sandpipers bob on the beach, and redpolls fly around in the scrub.

Redpoll

3 Return by the same path as far as the burn crossing. Look for hen harriers hunting over the moor. Before the path goes up the hill on the far side of the burn watch out for the stone with way-marks and turn left along a much smaller path. There is a post with a red-painted top some distance along this path. Fork right at a vague junction and climb through the bracken, passing a metal post, which has also been painted red. The path goes into trees and becomes clearer, and at the time of writing it is being cleared. It winds in and out through low birch and hazel trees; at another junction in a clearing keep right, as all the footprints do, to come out above the trees for a while. Then the path re-enters the wood and climbs up a gully on large stones, and here is the most enormous horizontal oak tree, said to be one of the oldest oaks on Mull. The path passes right underneath it. Come out at the top, cross open ground and go back into hazel woodland where the path goes down quite steeply. Then cross a valley, go up the far side and come out onto open moorland where you meet another path at another carved stone. Turn left and walk this wide easy path round the bottom of Torr Fada to rejoin your outward route and return to your car.

Marsh cinquefoil

Practicals

Type of walk: All on waymarked paths; the marks are mainly arrows carved into granite rocks and are therefore permanent but you have to look for them. Some of the paths are quite small and overgrown, although at the time of writing some clearing is taking place. The views, however, are excellent, there is a lot of interest, and the beach at the end is superb.

Total Distance:	6½ miles/10.5km
Time:	3–4 hours
Maps:	OS Explorer 373/Landranger 48

21

Erraid

Park as for Walk 20, or follow the road on through a gate to Knockvologan farm, where a field on the left before the farmhouse has a sign for car parking. To access this, drive along the minor road from Fionnphort past the Columba Visitor Centre to Knockvologan.

Erraid is well-known as the island where **David Balfour** was thrown ashore after being wrecked on the Torran Rocks in

Balfour Bay (Traigh Gheall), Erraid

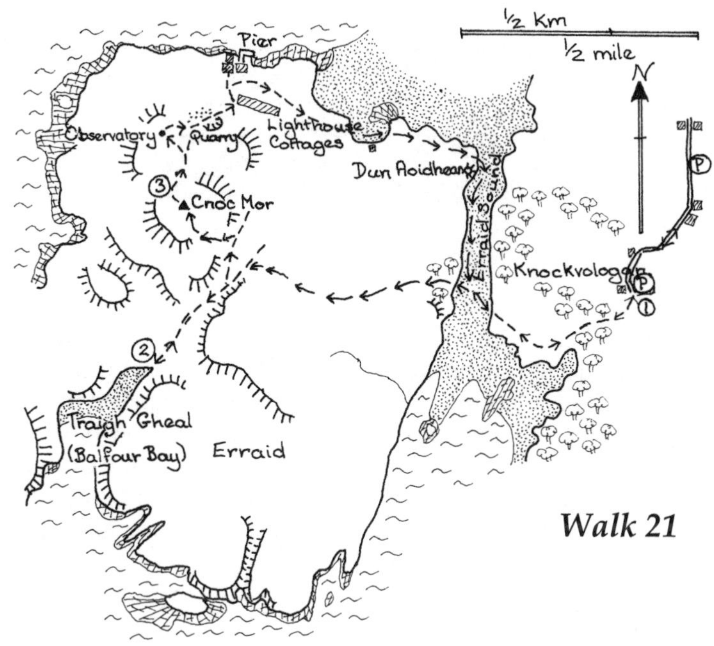

Robert Louis Stevenson's book 'Kidnapped'. The bay where he was washed up (Traigh Gheal) is now often called Balfour Bay. He was trapped for four days on the island, eating only shellfish, before discovering that it was a tidal island and he could walk off at low tide.

1 Walk on along the track from Knockvologan Farm as it descends through stunted woodland to the shore and comes out by a low pink granite cliff. Turn right along the sand and then go along a track running behind the beach through dunes to come out on the sand further along. Here if you have got your timing right there is dry sand right across to Erraid. Cross the sand and climb up a rock gully passing through scattered woodland; if the cows have been there it can be quite muddy. Continue up the gully and follow it as it bears slightly left. Cross a boggy area, then climb again. Carry on in the same general direction, using the frequent animal tracks, until the top of the highest hill on Erraid, Cnoc Mor, comes into view with a very obvious boulder on top. Aim for this until you reach a wide valley just before the

Brown hare

hill. Turn left here and join a good distinct path. The path keeps to the left side of the valley and goes close in under granite cliffs, where it crosses a couple of springs on stones. Then it moves out and goes down a steeper slope, with a white sand bay coming into view ahead. Cross three drains on small wooden bridges and walk over the short flowery turf to the bay. This is another Traigh Gheal (White Bay) also sometimes called called Balfour Bay and is surrounded by walls of pinkish granite. It is a wonderful place to eat a picnic, paddle, laze or explore – but don't forget about the tide.

2 Return by the same path until you have crossed the springs on stones. Then take a clear path off to the left across the bog and then uphill through bracken. Only follow it to the first shelf in the hillside and turn left here onto animal tracks. Make your way up into a narrow valley with two birch trees in a crag on the left. Climb easily out of the end of the valley, where the stone on top of Cnoc Mor becomes visible once more. Cross a boggy depression and climb steeply to reach it. The summit, marked by a cairn, is a few metres farther on. Enjoy the splendid view.

3 Below to the north you can see the small white-painted observatory. Take a path, which leads towards it. Keep right along the edge of higher ground at the first junction, then left at the next to go down into a valley. Carry on down until you are below the observatory, then climb steeply up to the left to reach it. Go in and see the prospect and details of Dubh Artach and Skerryvore lighthouses, then follow the good path leading straight down from the observatory. This winds right and comes down granite steps to the valley you left. Turn left and descend to a ruined house, which is unsafe. The path goes to the right and crosses the back of a quarry; huge granite blocks lie tumbled to the left. Go through a gate in a substantial wall and follow the path on down to join a track beside a row of cottages. Turn left, and go on for 55yds/50m then walk right through a gate onto a track which runs along below the cottage gardens. Go through a gate, or over a stile beside it, and carry on down the now grassy track to a beach. Cross the sand in front of a white cottage and then take to the grass again, winding along behind the shore on a clear path. Ahead to your right is a dun on a small granite knoll, and the path comes down to the shore again beside this. Walk along the channel between steep sides until you reach the point where you entered it. Find your outward path beside its wall of pink granite and walk back up to Knockvologan Farm.

Practicals

Type of walk: Erraid''s paths are mainly animal tracks, but from the old observatory there is a good track to the shore. Do not forget that it is a tidal island. Tide tables are available in Fionnphort, or you can get the information from www.ukho.gov.uk (select EasyTide and then click on Iona). Go across as soon as the channel is dry; how long you have will depend on the wind and whether it is spring or neap tides, but you should comfortably have 1½ hours either side of low tide, probably longer.

Total Distance: 4 miles/6.5km
Time: 2–3 hours
Maps: OS Explorer 373/Landranger 48

22

Ardalanish

Park in the well signed car park on the left of the road 55yds/50m before the road end, grid ref 373193. This is accessed by the A849 along the Ross of Mull to Bunessan. Here turn left along a minor road signed Uisken, with an additional sign for Ardalanish Weavers. (If you miss this turn there is another about 1 mile farther on). In ½ mile/1km turn left for Uisken, then after 1¼ miles/2km turn right, following the signs for Ardalanish Weavers.

The small **black Highland cattle** and the **Hebridean sheep** are ancient local breeds, possibly descended from Viking stock. Over hundreds of years they have developed in conjunction with the hill ecosystem; their grazing habits maintain the diversity of this fragile and difficult habitat. They also look after themselves better than lowland breeds, finding sheltered places on the hill in which to have their calves or lambs.

Ardalanish Bay

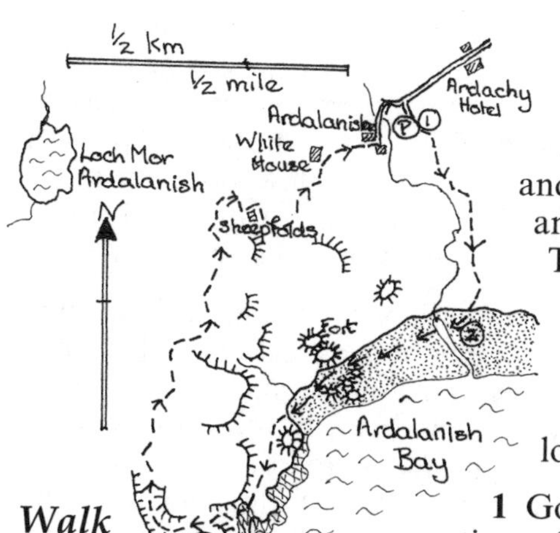

Walk 22

Ardalanish Farm is completely organic. The only fertilisers used on the fields are compost and seaweed, and all the winter fodder for the animals is grown on the farm. The wool from the sheep is woven in the weaving mill in the farmyard into attractive hardwearing garments and rugs; you are invited to look round.

1 Go down the track in the direction of the beach, through a gate and on along the pleasant grassy track bordered with flowery turf, full of wild carrot, eyebright, harebells, thyme and lady's bedstraw. Take a kissing gate beside a field gate where there is an information board describing the wildlife, machair and geology. Go on through the dunes to the wide silver sands where ringed plovers, curlews and oystercatchers feed at the water's edge and arctic terns fish out in the bay.

2 Walk right along the sands, to reach an area of huge boulders and rocky stacks. Wind between them (this may be difficult at high tide) and when your way is finally blocked by rocks climb a stile over the fence at the top of the beach. A faded sign asks you not to take dogs. Keep left along a narrow path running through the vegetation behind craggy rocks, until you reach another bay and the grass ends. Carry on over or between boulders below a low cliff to arrive at a grassy gully. Step up quite steeply onto a small

Thyme

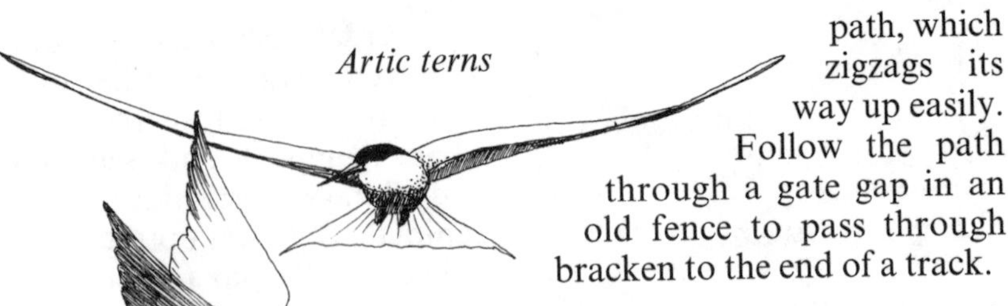
Artic terns

path, which zigzags its way up easily. Follow the path through a gate gap in an old fence to pass through bracken to the end of a track.

3 Walk on along the track through a narrow craggy defile until it joins another at a T-junction. The steep-sided rocky eminence over to the left is marked as a dun on the map, but reaching the summit must have been a problem. Turn right, and walk the pleasant high level track as it winds between the knolls and crags; there is a lovely view through gaps to the bay, backed by the distant Carsaig cliffs, on your right. Soon Ardalanish Loch appears on your left. Small black Highland cattle and very black Hebridean sheep feed beside the track. Go through a gate; a sign on the far side marks the end of the farm trail and there is an arrow to a viewpoint where you will find a wooden seat. After a pause here, return to the trail and continue on down past cattle pens and then into fields. Go by the white house and on down to the farm buildings. Here you will find the woollen mill and a small shop, also from 2008 a café. Then go ahead down the access road, through a gate and on 55yds/50m to turn right into the car park.

Practicals

Type of walk: A delightful ramble, mostly on tracks and the beach, with one short awkward bit where you have to scramble over and between boulders. At high spring tides the beach part may be inaccessible.

Total Distance:	2 miles/3.4km
Time:	1½ hours
Map:	OS Explorer 373/Landranger 48
NB:	Remember to check times of high tides.

23a

Carsaig Arches

Park at Carsaig Pier, grid ref 545 213 where there is limited parking for 5 or 6 cars, parked carefully. Best get there early as this is a popular walk. To access the pier, turn south off the A849 Ross of Mull road at Pennyghael, along a very minor road which goes over the Ross and steeply down to Carsaig. At a fork on the way down take the left branch signed to Inniemore and Carsaig Pier.

The **Nuns' Cave** is wide and shallow and is said to have been the temporary home of nuns from Iona who were expelled from

Carsaig Arches

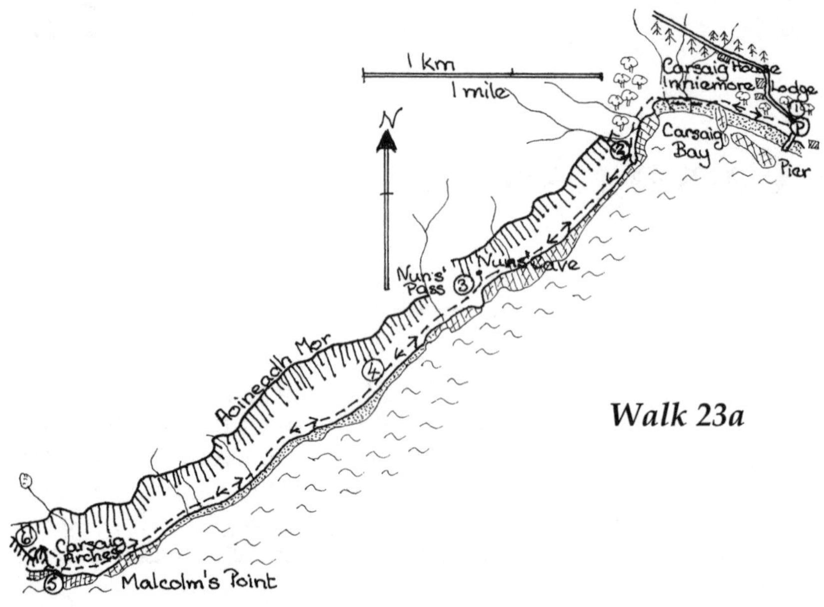

Walk 23a

the island during the reformation. There are ancient carvings on the walls, crosses, and masons' marks, and a sailing ship plus modern graffiti. The sandstone slabs in front of the cave were quarried for building; some were used for Iona Abbey.

The **Carsaig Arches** are two spectacular rock arches, where caves eroded into the columnar basalt cliffs have worn right through. The first one is huge with the sea lapping into one end of it. The second one is much narrower, a hole pierced through a thin stack, which is detached from the cliff. Beyond is a table-like slab called Leac nan Leum, the slab of the leap.

1 Return up the road for a few yards/metres from the parking area and go down a track on the left. This runs beside a wall and is overhung with lime trees that line the bank beyond the wall. Where it forks, take the left branch, passing through a gap between the gate and the wall, and carry on along the back of the beach on a pleasant raised grassy path. The path then runs into gorse and comes to a locked gate with a stile and a notice saying all dogs must be on leads. Do not cross the stile but follow one of the little paths that leads down onto the shore; cross the pebbles and walk along the firm grey sand. Ford two burns, usually easier to do farther down the beach, and make your way back up onto the grassy flats at the back of the beach. Continue along the good path, with occasional wet patches, which you can get round or over, using planks placed by previous walkers.

2 Go through a metal kissing gate in a wall and carry on along the path, which soon becomes stony. Look for otters fishing offshore in the multitude of tidal inslets, and for feral goats with magnificent horns which live all along this coast. The path runs behind or sometimes above the beach. Soon it climbs steeply to cross a recent rockfall. If you don't like the look of the steep scree climb go down onto the beach and make your way across the pebbles; this is slower but easier. The continuing path is distinct but often rocky and crosses boulder fields where you have to pick your way carefully. It is not a quick walk.

3 After 1½ miles/2.5km and about one hour's walking you reach an area where there are great flat sandstone slabs lining the foreshore, and two craggy rocks rearing up ahead. Look for a small path leading up steeply on the right, and go up it to the Nuns' Cave and see the carvings. Then return to the shore path and walk on, past the steep grassy break in the cliffs called the Nuns' Pass. Then follow the path as it climbs high, this time because the middle of the old good path has been washed out. Either climb above it or again take to the beach and make your way quite easily between huge boulders until you can rejoin the path.

Wild Goats

Black Guillemot

4 After this the going becomes easier for a while along the base of a grassy slope bright with flowers in summer. You may see a peregrine fly out from the cliffs with powerful wing beats. The good path then reverts to stones and you need to go along the beach again to avoid a badly eroded area. The shore changes from pebbles and boulders to rocks, with dramatic inlets and stacks, and you know you are getting near your destination. Round a corner you can see the first arch. Cross the beach towards it and climb onto a rough black basalt outcrop, and there below you is a deep inlet blocking further progress. The huge arch is across the far side, with sea lapping into the nearest side. You can see right through to the beach beyond, but cannot get there.

5 To see the second arch, experienced walkers with a good head for heights should go back a few steps to a stream channel, which may be dry, and climb up its grassy, stony bank until a clear goat path goes off left. This takes you precariously above the inlet, with a sheer drop to your left, and on above the arch, then once over the crest it turns sharply right and curves round the base of a rocky amphitheatre, coming down gently to the beach. The whole path is very exposed and you must not slip, but once over the crest it feels better. The second arch, narrow and spectacular, is joined to the cliff by a rocky causeway. It is possible to stand under both arches from this beach. Black guillemots nest in holes in the cliffs and constantly fly in from the sea, and shags stand on the lower rocks.

6 Explore the amazing rocks; then you have to return over the narrow exposed path and walk back the long four miles to the pier.

Field gentian

Practicals

Type of walk: There is a clear path all the way but sometimes it crosses rockfalls and in several cases it is easier to go down onto the beach to make your way round these. The walking is not particularly easy and you will need most of the day to get all the way to the arches and back, unless you are very fit and agile. The final stretch over the cliff to the second arch is very narrow and vertiginous. All the walk is spectacular and if you only get to see the first arch it is worth doing.

Total Distance:	8 miles/13km to the arches and back; to the Nuns' Cave and back 3 miles/5km
Time:	6 hours or 2 hours
Maps:	OS Explorer 375 and 373/Landranger 48

23b

Carsaig to An Dunan

Parking and access as for Carsaig Arches, walk 23a.

An Dunan is a basalt stack which has been cut out from the cliffs by the sea when sea levels were higher after the last ice age. The name means a fort, but it is doubtful whether it was ever used as one because of its inaccessibility. The caves, of which there are several on this walk, are also relics of higher sea levels.

Geological dykes are formed when molten material is squeezed into cracks in the already existing rocks, and then solidifies. They cut across the strata of the original rocks. Similar structures parallel to the strata are called sills. Sometimes dykes are harder than the surrounding rock, in which case they remain standing out as the rock weathers and is worn away. The two visible on the beach below the path stand up like this. In other cases the rock of the dyke is softer and weathers out to form a groove.

An Dunan

Walk 23b

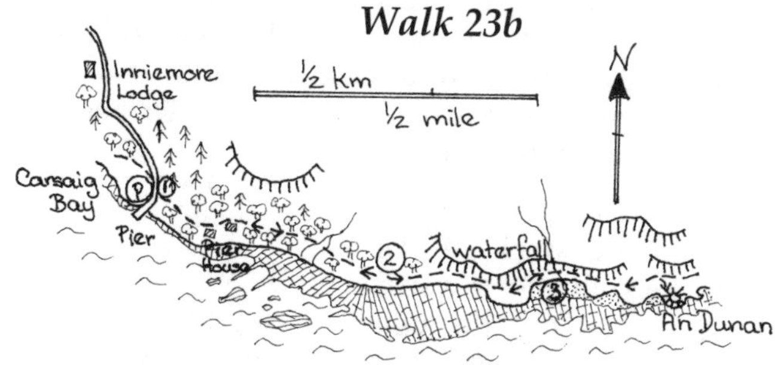

1 Walk a few steps uphill from the pier and turn right along a track with a sign 'Public Footpath to Lochbuie' and also signed for Pier Cottage and the Library. At the gate to Pier Cottage go left round outside the fence, and again at the next gate. Follow the lovely path through mature woodland on a shelf above the sea, then go down to a wide grassy area with irises and later, spotted orchids. Boggy bits can be crossed on planks. Cross a burn and go into woodland again, this time mainly birch and hazel but with a mixture of other trees. When you leave the trees the path runs along a shelf again, with wonderful flowery grassland to your left but unfortunately bracken to your right. Look down at the shore to see wide sandstone slabs with two raised igneous dykes cutting across them and also across each other.

2 Go through another small wood to come out below cliffs. These are not as high as on the other side of Carsaig Bay. The beach here is littered with huge boulders fallen from above and the path keeps close to the base of the cliff, where there are several caves in the cliff. The first is large and lies up a steep slope, with a roofless gully to its left. Round a corner is a lower much deeper cave. Carry on along the path, which goes across the pebbles heading for a waterfall, falling the full length of the cliff, making a delicate curtain over the front of a third narrow cave. Cross the burn below it and

Yellowhammer

then keep beside the cliff to reach the fourth cave, very low in the base. Stroll on along the path, which has been built up here for several yards/metres. Oystercatchers shout from the beach below, red-throated divers wail out on the water and groups of yellowhammers feed on seeds.

3 Round the next corner you can see the dramatic stack of An Dunan. Make your way towards it winding in and out through more huge boulders, until you reach the fine grassy sward joining it to the cliffs. Go across and look at it. It is a huge lump of basalt, with some of the characteristic organ pipe structure, and there is a cave, with a wall partly across the entrance, on the landward side.This is a fine place to explore. The view across the mouth of Loch Buie is also very good. It is possible to walk right round to Lochbuie but you would have to arrange transport for the other end. It is easier to return the way you came.

Heath Spotted Orchid

Practicals

Type of walk: An easy short walk, mostly on paths although they become rather lost sometimes on the beach sections. The views are very good and the coast exciting.

Total Distance: 2 miles/3.4km
Time: 1–2 hours
Maps: OS Explorer 375/Landranger 48

24

Lochbuie to Glenbyre

Park on the small parking area, overlooking the sea, opposite Lochbuie post office, grid ref 608249. To reach this take the A849 south along the side of Loch Spelve and, at Strathcoil, turn left to take a narrow road that continues beside the large loch. Continue ahead beside Loch Uisg, soon to arrive at the parking area at Lochbuie.

By day the **woodcock** shuns the daylight, crouching quietly in woodland, its colour and markings blending in with the surroundings, making it invisible unless disturbed. Then it rises with a swish of wings, and dodges, low, through the trees to drop at a safe distance. At dusk the bird leaves the woodland to feed in

Glenbyre

marshes and muddy ditches where the ground is soft in which to push its long sensitive bill for worms.

Loch Buie is a wide inlet in the cliff-bound south coast that allowed sea access. It has fertile flats at the head of the loch.

1 Walk on for a quarter of a mile to the end of the road, where you cross a delightful new bridge. Turn right up the farm track to the signposted Cameron farm, a white dwelling tucked under the lower, southern slopes of Ben Buie. Pass through a gate, bear right and then curve left, to pass through another before the farmhouse. Climb the track through vast areas of bracken where foxgloves and yellow flags poke through the green mantle. Go past a picturesque ruined crofthouse and carry on through a gate to its right. Carry on soon to ascend through oak, rowan, birch and hazel. Follow the undulating path as it heads towards the foot of Beinn nan Gobhar. Cross through a barrier pole in a wall gap and then use stones to cross a burn gathering its water high up on the slopes.

2 Climb a little right, then winding left, go on parallel with a wall on your left. Where the path divides (rather indistinct) ignore the branch climbing steeply to the pass over the hills to Rossal at the head of Loch Scridain. Walk on along the lower path, which moves into bracken but soon becomes more distinct as it comes

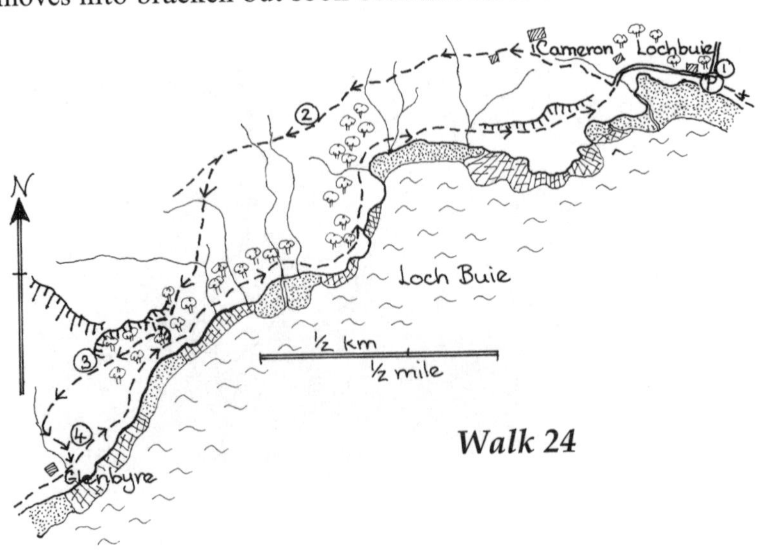

Walk 24

Woodcock

closer to the wall on your left. Where the wall turns away, left, go on ahead up a slope, soon to leave the ubiquitous bracken behind. After a little descent the path crosses a burn and then moves into ancient deciduous woodland. Walk on along the high-level, shelf-like path, from where through the leafy foliage, you can see the sparkling water of Loch Buie, far below. As you stroll on, go quietly as you might disturb a pair of woodcocks resting in the vegetation beside the path. After a narrow landslip, which you should cross with care, the path becomes wider but alas, in summer, the bracken higher.

3 Once the trees are left behind the path continues through more bracken and is still very high on the slopes of Beinn nan Gobhar. Eventually you reach a large boulder in a grassy clearing. Pause here and look out to sea to enjoy the pleasing view. Then stroll on the narrow path through more bracken. When you reach an indistinct division of the way, ignore the branch that leads off up Glen Byre and carry on along the lower path, which gently descends, until the bracken ends. Continue ahead for a few steps and then wind downhill, using mainly animal tracks. Soon, look for the fine chimney pots of the derelict farmhouse of Glen Byre on the shore. Follow the faint path as it gradually descends, winding left above the building. Towards the shore there are some easy rocky outcrops to scramble down, but remember to look before you descend.

4 Turn left to begin your return along the good access track that keeps parallel with the shoreline. This is a delight to stride after your adventures higher up the slopes. Look as you go for the many caves at the foot of the high cliffs. Look for storm beaches where the waves have thrown an enormous amount of large stones across the track. Enjoy, in summer, the glorious floral display, which delight many butterflies and dragonflies, also the multitude of small streams which descend the steep cliffs passing through sheer rock gullies. Continue on the lovely way until you reach the new bridge once more and carry on to the parking area. Here, out in the bay, you might spot red-throated divers.

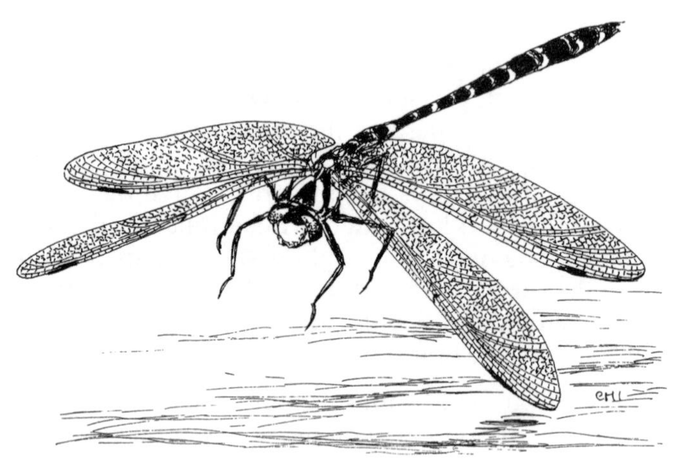

Golden-ringed Dragonfly

Practicals

Type of walk: A glorious walk of great contrasts. Pleasing to do before the bracken emerges, but even at its height, the paths are still visible. The high-level path was the original access to Glenbyre before the shore path was put in.

Total Distance:	4 miles/6.5km
Time:	3 hours
Maps:	OS Explorer 375/Landranger 49 & 48

25

Lochbuie, Moy Castle, Laggan

Park as for walk 24. If the parking area is full, turn left along track by the shore and park opposite the church, grid ref 609247.

The early 15th century **Moy Castle** is believed to have been built by Hector MacLean. At ground level the family had a well of fresh water. Above were two more storeys and a garret. The castle was taken over during the Civil War and soldiers were garrisoned in it. Eventually it was returned to the MacLeans who abandoned it for their new house, in the 1750s. Today it stands, a romantic ruin.

1 Walk east from the Post Office along the shore track, with the sea to your right. Soon you reach a substantial house with a tiny church, the Church of St Kilda, tucked behind it. Carry on along

Stone Circle, Lochbuie

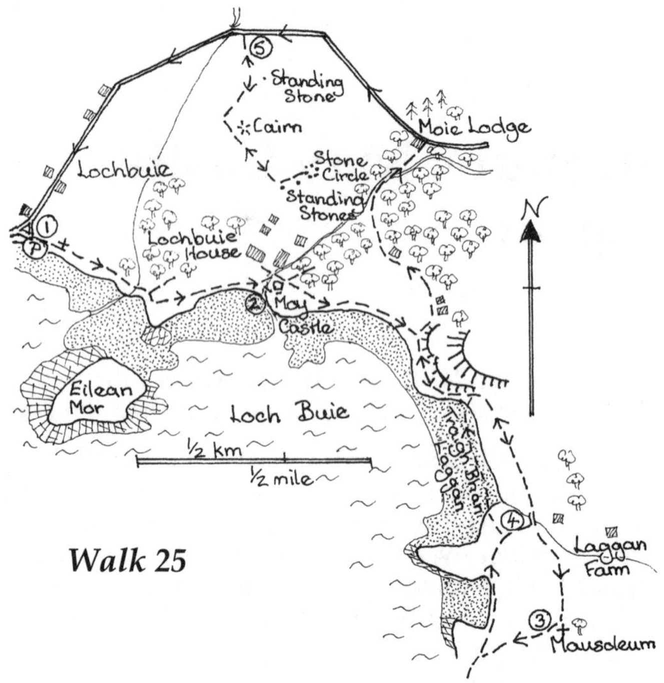

Walk 25

the track, past a notice stating that it is the private drive to Lochbuie House but also the footpath to Moy Castle and Laggan Sands. Cross the hump-backed bridge and immediately turn right, as directed, round an iron gate. Head left to cross the grass at the back of the shore, go over a small burn and walk in front of the large house. At the Y-junction take the right turn, signed Moy Castle. Cross a footbridge to see the imposing ruin, which at the time of writing is being 'done up' or made safe, courtesy of Historic Scotland.

2 Return over the footbridge and turn right to go through a gate and out onto a track. Walk right and, at a cross of tracks 55yds/50m further on turn right again, signed for Laggan Sands. The track runs above the shore with a haymeadow full of flowers on the left. Branch right at a T-junction onto a track, which winds round, cut out of the cliff above the shore. Ahead is the wide expanse of Laggan Sands, clean and beautiful. The track runs over grass at the back of the beach. Where it turns left to Laggan Farm, continue ahead on a grassier track. Cross a

Fallow deer

burn and wind left up to the top of a river terrace, and walk on to a chapel and mausoleum in a clump of trees ahead. The mausoleum was built for the MacLaines (a branch of the MacLeans), and has been recently restored. You will want to wander around here.

3 On leaving, turn left outside the wall and pick up an animal track, which crosses the pasture to a gate in the far left corner. You can follow the continuing track across grass and over a burn, then wind on out towards the headland. But if you would rather leave this to another day, turn right immediately and go through an old iron gate beside another gate and follow the track back towards the sands. As you go, listen for snipe drumming overhead, oystercatchers and common sandpipers calling from the rocks along the shore and you may also hear the plaintive call of a golden plover.

4 Rejoin your outward path by the bridge over the burn, or ford it lower down and walk back across the sands to rejoin the track before the craggy outcrop. At the T-junction walk straight on, passing two cottages and then a third on the right. The track then passes into splendid mature beech woods. Ignore a path to the left, cross a burn and come out to the road, through white gates by Moie Lodge. Walk left along the road with care. There is little traffic but for the first 110yds/100m there is not much of a verge. As you go look for fallow deer in the woods and red deer to your right on the hill. At a small car park before a bridge over the Abhainn a' Chaiginn Mhoir, turn left as directed for the stone circle, the only one in Mull.

5 Go through the metal kissing gate beside the farm gate. Walk ahead over rather damp pasture, following the white-painted stones. Cross a little bridge and carry on until you reach a fence. Turn left and continue down beside the fence, now on your right. At the fence corner, walk left to pass through a deer gate a few yards along. A notice asks you to close the gates. Beyond, to the left, is the very fine stone circle, set in a green pasture, with one standing stone set apart. You will want to linger in this lovely corner. There is another stone by the last corner and there is one more in the field first crossed. Return by your outward route to the road and walk left for the last half mile to return to the car park.

Ragged Robin and Lady's Smock

Practicals

Type of walk: Most pleasing. Level, easy, on tracks and some road walking.

Total Distance:	5 miles/8km
Time:	2½ hours plus time on beach
Map:	OS Explorer 375/Landranger 49 & 48

26

Port Donain

Park only in the small car park (space for 4 or 5 cars) on the right about 0.5km from Grass Point, grid ref 744303. To access this, if coming from Craignure, turn left off the A849 just past Lochdon, signed Grass Point. There are several signs saying the road is narrow with few passing places and parking places.

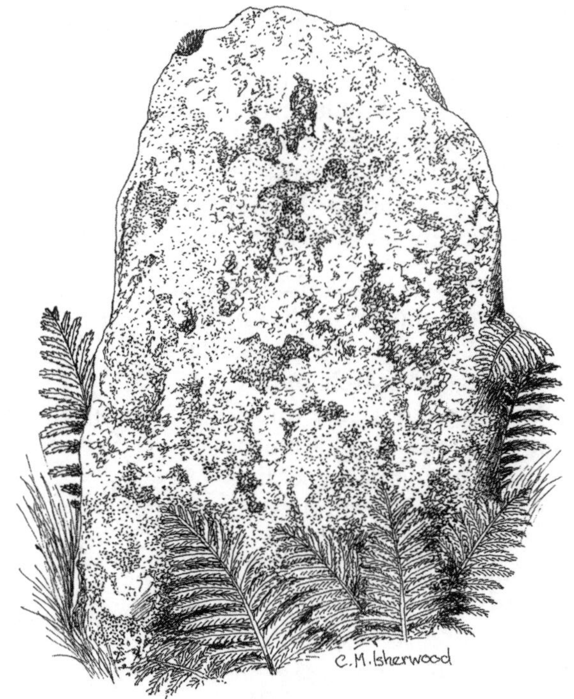

Chambered Cairn, Port Donain

Grass Point, at the end of the road, was once the main ferry port from Mull for Oban; it is the nearest point to the mainland and all the cattle that were exported from the island went from here. Before you set off, walk along to see the old harbour.

1 From the parking area, return up the road to the farm at Auchnacraig and go through its entrance into the yard. Turn right and pass through a gate between two barns. Beyond the gate ahead, follow a track to a deer gate with an interesting pin to fasten it. Carry on to where the track divides and take the right branch, which goes round the back (west) of a little knoll, Cnoc an't-Seana-bhaile, where you might spot red deer. The track divides again several times; always take the right hand one, keeping below the rocky knoll. Continue down through oak trees beside a small burn. The track then divides once more and here take the left fork which cuts through an old settlement boundary wall, and look for the chambered cairns. The first is hard to see because of the bracken, but then you reach a much clearer track and a second cairn stands beside it. Follow this track round to the right and down to a lovely sandy beach.

2 Stroll over the beach, cross the burn at the far south end and go up to another path. If you wish to see the old settlement you will need to search among the bracken. Go through a gate and follow the shoreline round on a reasonably easy path but which becomes increasingly vague. Eventually it degenerates into animal tracks made by wild goats and deer and continues for a short way along a wave-cut platform, cut off from the shore by low cliffs.

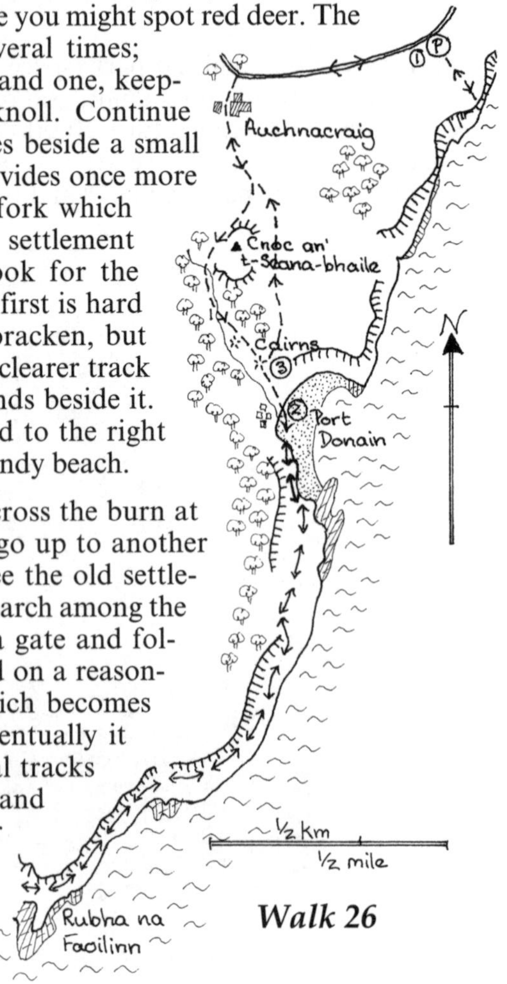

Walk 26

As soon as trees start appearing to the left, take an easy way down to the lower ground. Follow this and make your way behind the shore, using more animal tracks. Notice the increasingly interesting rock formations on the right. Scramble easily over two prominent boundary walls, to reach the promontory of Rubha na Faoilinn, from where there are excellent views of the islands to the south, and up Loch Spelve. You may wish to continue along the shore to look for the ruined settlement of Gortenanrue up above the next bay. Then return by your outward route towards Port Donain.

3 At the chambered cairn above Port Donain go ahead, passing round the other side (east) of Cnoc an't-Seana-bhaile and follow clear tracks back to the farm. Return to the car park, where you may like to take an interesting diversion along a small path (south) beaten into the vegetation behind the car park and then along the top of the cliffs. There are very good panoramic views, particularly up Loch Linnhe, and across to Duart Castle. Quite soon the path stops at a point overlooking wooded cliffs. Go back down to the car park by the same route.

Red deer hind

Practicals

Type of walk: As this interesting ramble is along an unfrequented piece of coast walking is not always easy and some route finding is required, but there is always the shore for a guideline. Port Donain is a lovely beach and the views from the headland are fine.

Total Distance: 5 miles/8km
Time: 3 hours
Maps: OS Explorer 375/Landranger 49

Craignure and Torosay

Park in the large free car park beside the road in Craignure, just south of the Caledonian MacBrayne ferry pier, grid ref 719370. Access is by the A849.

Torosay Castle was designed, in 1858, by David Bryce in Scottish Baronial style. The 12 acres of gardens include formal Italianate terraces and the famous statue walk laid out by Sir Robert Lorrimer in 1899, which contrasts pleasingly with the dramatic scenery all around. The journey on the Isle of Mull narrow gauge passenger railway from Craignure to Torosay by diesel or steam, takes 20 minutes.

1 From the car park, cross the road and grass opposite to walk right along a small footpath. Come out opposite the Craignure

Torosay Castle

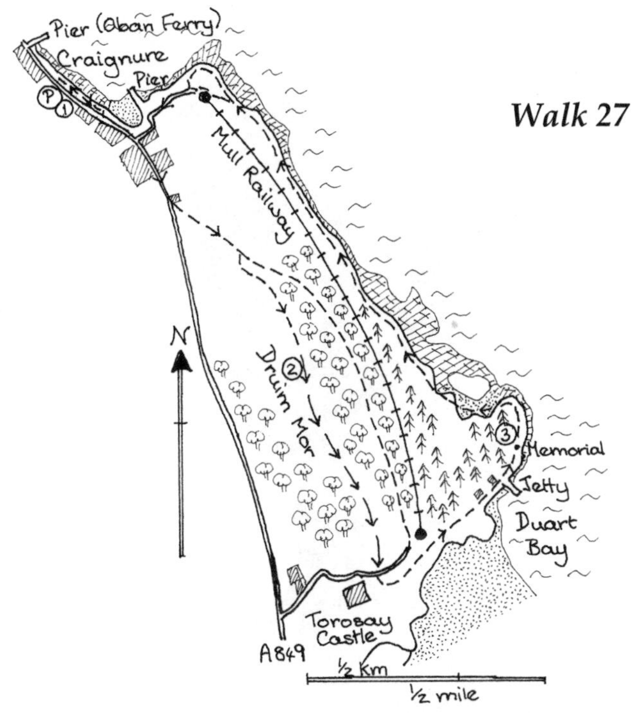

Walk 27

Inn and carry on along the pavement uphill to the derestriction sign. Turn left through gateposts beside a white painted cottage (Torosay North Lodge); the sign says 'Forest Walk to Torosay Castle 1 mile'. Walk on through mature trees and then beside a meadow on the left. You are likely to see rabbits and maybe a greater spotted woodpecker. Take a branch track to the right, which swings round parallel to the original track but climbs up above it, through a gate and on to a telecommunications mast on top of the hill. The track stops here. Make your way left round the fence through a narrow gap; it's a little wet at first but soon improves. Move right at the end of the fence to reach the crest of the hill. There are lovely views of Morvern and Loch Linnhe with Lismore across its mouth, and Duart Castle on the next headland south.

2 Walk down the field to pass through a gate where the field is constricted between two woods. Go on down the next field, with a fine view of the castle, and bear slightly right to go through a

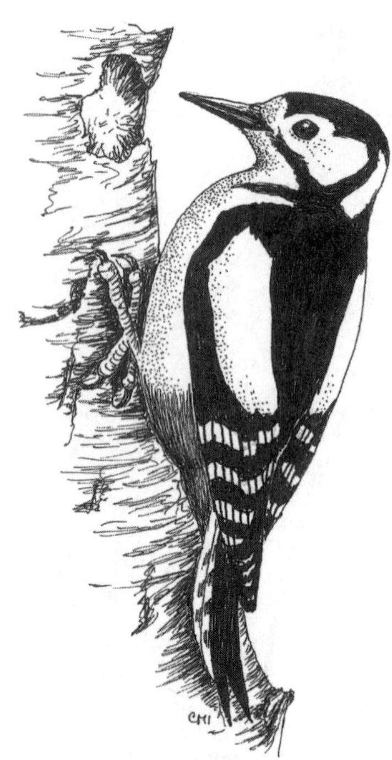

Great Spotted Woodpecker

little wicket gate in the fence at the bottom onto a road. Turn right and carry straight on, if you wish to visit the house and gardens. Otherwise turn left to walk down a track signed to the Mull Railway, past the car park, and then past the railway terminus (you may wish to return to Craignure by rail) and on towards the shore. Go by a cottage and then a boathouse by a little jetty, and up steps at the far side. There are common sandpipers along the shore, and a good view across the bay to Duart Castle. Continue on the path, through pines and then a metal gate to a Celtic Cross Memorial to Murray Guthrie, who purchased Torosay Castle in 1875, and members of his family.

3 Cross the open space, go through another gate and follow the narrow path as it winds round above the shore. Cross the head of a little inlet, then a saltmarsh where the turf is full of thrift and sea asters (this part could be difficult at high spring tides). The path alternates between saltmarsh and the grass and iris beds behind, sometimes crossing pebbles high on the beach. Look for limestone slabs full of fossil shells. Otters use this beach and if you are quiet you may see one. The path divides and rejoins and although small in places it always goes on. As you approach Craignure the path becomes wider and more well-defined. Then you can see the first houses, and the signal at the end of the Mull Railway. Two paths cut off to the left across the bog but you are probably as well to stay just above the shore until you have rounded the point and then head left up to the end of the railway line. Walk round the fence to join the road, and follow it into Craignure, where you turn right at the main road to return to your car.

Thrift

Practicals

Type of walk: Short and very pleasant, which you can extend by visiting the house and gardens. The return above the shore is delightful (although probably best avoided at high spring tides), and there is always the chance of seeing an otter.

Total Distance:	2½ miles/4km
Time:	1–2 hours plus time spent in the castle and gardens
Maps:	OS Explorer 375/Landranger 49

28

Dun da Ghaoithe

Scallastle River and Dun da Ghaoithe

Park as for Walk 27.

Dun da Ghaoithe, 2512ft/766m, means Fort of the two Winds, and its position above the Sound of Mull probably justifies the name. It is the only Corbett on Mull; a Corbett is a hill between 2,500ft/762m and 3,000ft/914.4m, with at least a 500ft/150m drop between it and any higher top. Although from below it appears somewhat disfigured by the prominent communications installations, once above them and on the ridge they can be forgotten and the fine views enjoyed to the full. The track to the installations does provide an easy climb for much of the way up.

1 Cross the road from the car park and go over the grass to a footpath

Walk 28

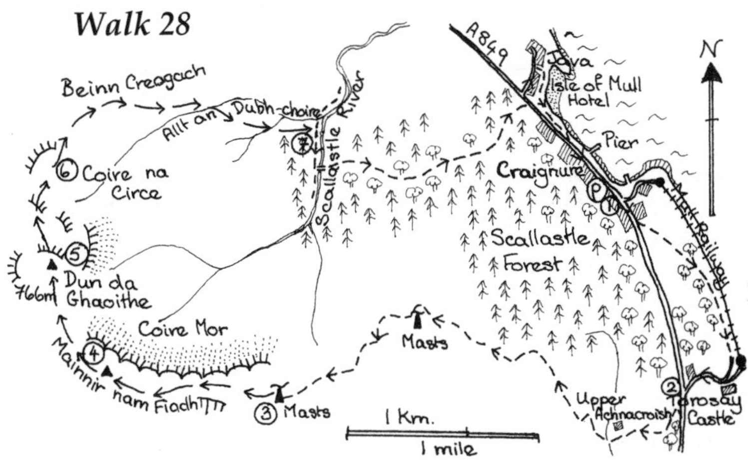

where you turn right. Continue ahead when you rejoin the pavement and walk uphill beside the main road leading south out of Craignure. Go past the Craignure Inn and the Church. Then go through a gateway, on the left, with a white cottage beside it, and a sign by the track saying 'Forest Walk to Torosay Castle'. Follow the lovely track through mature deciduous woodland. As an alternative, and to save you a mile of walking, you could take the Mull Railway to reach Torosay Castle. At the end of the track walk right, past the castle, and out down the drive to the main road.

2 Bear left and walk carefully along the verge for 220yds/200m. Then cross the road and turn right into the approach road for the Bird of Prey Centre. Ignore a road on the left and wind round uphill through fine mature oak trees all hung with lichens and epiphytic ferns. Go past the car park and then the road to the centre and carry on along the track to a gate. Cross the fence by a tall metal ladder stile and begin the long climb up to the communications complex. The track is easy to follow and to walk, although rather hard on the feet. The views out across Loch Linnhe are superb. Go past a group of huge masts and then on, for a further mile, to reach another. Here the track ends.

3 Go on up the ridge; the way is clear enough although there are no definitive paths, just bits of ones. Cross several narrow rocky ridges and follow the edge of the huge corrie, Coire Mor, climbing steadily over pleasant short grass and moss. Higher up the ridge becomes stonier. Finally you reach a summit crowned with a huge heap of stones like a burial cairn; this summit is Mainnir nam Fiadh, almost but not quite as high as the main top. There is a cylindrical trig point here as well as the cairn.

4 Descend into the dip beyond this top and then climb the increasingly stony ridge round the edge of the corrie to reach the actual summit, Dun da Gaoithe, also surmounted by a huge cairn. The view from here is stunning, generally held to be one of the best in Mull. Not only can you see all the mainland hills beyond Loch Linnhe, but all the Mull mountains seem near at hand; to the south you can glimpse Jura and Scarba and to the north beyond Ardnamurchan are Rum and Eigg.

5 During the stalking season or if the weather is closing in you will have to return by your ascent route. However if you feel more adventurous, climb over the small rocky ridge on which the cairn sits and walk on down the fine ridge. About 0.5km farther on bear right to leave the main ridge and take another, Beinn Creagach, which encloses Coire na Circe. The walking is still excellent over short turf with areas of pebbles and terraces where starry saxifrage and dwarf willows grow. Near the top of the ridge are three narrow rock bands; all have easy ways through them but you do have to look for them. Look around from time

Starry Saxifrage

Golden eagle

to time; you may spot an eagle soaring above the hill, or a mountain hare running easily across rough ground.

6 Walk on along the ridge over bumps and hollows, descending steadily until you come to a deeper depression with a rocky knoll on the far side. Turn right in the bottom and make your way down into the corrie, then follow a small path along the near bank of the burn, the Allt an Dubh-choire, which has several fine waterfalls. Listen for the plaintive calls of golden plovers. Continue beside the burn to a fence, cross the water on stones and go through a gate in the fence. Here all semblance of a path disappears. Make your way down with the Allt an Dubh-choire to your left, heading for the lower edge of Scallastle Forest. It is only about ½ mile/1km but the going is not easy, through alternate bracken and purple moor grass, which makes tussocks and is boggy. Go carefully over this ankle-twisting stretch. Lower down there is a fence, on the right, and walkers have made a small path beside it which helps your descent.

7 Descend to a track and turn right to go through a gate. Follow the rather overgrown way beyond until it joins another track by a footbridge over the Scallastle Burn. Turn left and cross the bridge, then climb the good path into the open deciduous woodland. Keep left at a junction. The forest is being returned to native trees and there are signs at intervals to tell you about it.

Go through clear-fell followed by conifers and then the path turns into a forest track down past the car park to the main road. You can turn right and walk along the pavement into Craignure, but a pleasanter way is to turn left and then immediately right into a road which goes past the Isle of Mull Hotel to a group of houses called Java. Turn right here down a side road ending in a path, which swings right to follow the shore all the way back to Craignure. Then stroll the pavement to the car park.

Dwarf willow

Practicals

Type of walk: The climb up Dun da Ghaoithe is easy, on a track and then over stony ground and short turf. The walk along the surprisingly narrow ridge is delightful, and the descent route is very pleasant until you reach the pathless section, which is mercifully short. This is a long walk although if you take the train at the start you can save one mile. The views are superb. In the stalking season you are asked to return by our route of ascent.

Total Distance:	11 miles/17km
Time:	5–6 hours
Maps:	OS Explorer 375/ Landranger 49

29

Iona – north

Park in the pay-and-display car park close to the ferry at Fionnphort at the end of the Ross, grid ref 300234. There is extra parking above this on the right side of the A849. There is also a large free car park by the Columba Centre.

Iona lies a mile off the Ross of Mull. A regular Caledonian MacBrayne ferry service takes you across from Fionnphort to The Village, Baile Mor. Cars are only carried if they have a special permit.

The **corncrake** is a slender, brown, short-billed bird, with barred sides and rich chestnut wings. It is a bird whose rasping call is heard only in the Hebrides and Orkney; it is rarely seen. It commonly nests in hay meadows but sometimes chooses a wetter situation such as an iris bed. The nest is a grass lined hollow and

The Nunnery, Iona

Walk 29

at times the surrounding blades of grass are bent over to help concealment. It has become seriously rare because of the trend for making silage (the grass is cut earlier), instead of hay, when many nests and chicks are destroyed. However farmers in the Hebrides and Orkney are working with the RSPB to help the corncrakes by cutting their crop later, after the chicks are hatched and fledged, and numbers are increasing in these areas.

1 From the ferry slipway walk ahead to take the second turn on the right to pass the 12th century Nunnery and then the Abbey. Ignore the footpath to Dun I and carry on to the end of the metalled road. Pass through two kissing gates, ignoring the track on the right to the farm, and a farm track to the left. From here you have an excellent view of Mull, the Ardnamurchan peninsula, the Treshnish islands, with the island of Rum in the distance. As you continue listen for evocative calls of corncrakes in the haymeadows. The path continues delightfully downhill towards the north shore. Go through a gate at the end of the track and walk across the lovely sandy bay. Many of the rocks about the shore have 'streams' of green and red serpentine in them. If the tide is out you can walk the shore or, if not, climb up a few rocks at the top of the sands to reach a pleasing grassy path that runs above the beach. Step over a little wire fence and continue to the end of a second beach of very fine sand – a great delight.

2 Head on to the top left corner of this bay and climb up the first of several little gullies onto a higher grassy open area. Look for a narrow path going on ahead, with the sea to the right and Dun I away to the left. Cross a fine meadow, and follow the path as it winds round slightly left of some rocky outcrops to reach a fence, with a gate. Go through and curve, slightly right, avoiding a boggy hollow full of cotton grass. Then pick up the little path that goes on ahead, soon to arc round a higher part of the boggy basin, this time keeping to the left side. Leave by the left hand corner of this area on a slightly ascending path that crosses, right, and then winds round the next bog on its right side, where the little path takes you over several low outcrops. Edge the continuing outcrops on your right. Follow the faint path as it crosses, keeping almost level, above a wide ravine descending to the sea. Look for a perched boulder away to your left.

3 On reaching a derelict wall, go through it and bear right almost to its end. Then head across a small valley through which runs a little stream, racing towards a deep water sea inlet far below. Climb the slope ahead, between gneiss outcrops, and keep to the side of more outcrops, on the left. The faint path occasionally disappears and then emerges a short distance along. As you edge the next wet area, watch out for where previous walkers have stepped up on a low rock to avoid a small wet patch, above a deep natural spring, hidden by moss. Then the path goes uphill, winding left of more outcrops, and finally begins to descend to a fence. Hopefully you have arrived where two fence posts with pointed tops are closer together than others, and where the strand of wire between them is free of barbs.

Corncrake

4 Step over and cross the stream, below, on stones. Ahead is an ancient wall traversing the slopes and another running up the fell. Pass through the wall directly ahead and continue up the path, keeping parallel with the wall on your left. Edge the rocky outcrops, up and up, on the left, and then go up over a huge buttercup meadow, with a hillfort on the high hill, directly ahead. Approach the Dun on its left side. Climb the path up the 'nose' of the hill and start winding round outcrops and ascending the grassy areas in between. Zig-zag up to the summit, all very easy, to enjoy the superb view down to the Back of the Ocean Bay and all the nearby magnificent stacks and little bays.

5 Descend by the same route and carry on, keeping on a vehicle track that hugs the foot of the hill. Follow the track as it winds on left and then look for a narrow path, dropping right down the sandy slopes through the marram grass, to cross a narrow burn. Carry on to a fine sandy bay, which you cross and leave by the far left corner. Wind over another glorious buttercup meadow towards a stile, with the sea to your right.

6 Climb the stile and go ahead on the fine turf beside a fence to your left, with the first house of The Village coming into view. Head left towards a track you can see rising over the hill. Join the track, which eventually reaches a gate and beyond a metalled road continues all the way to the shore. It then bears left to arrive at the pier.

Practicals

Type of walk: A challenging lovely walk, best done after a dry spell of weather. There are little paths to follow but sometimes these are not always easy to spot. Some of the paths are poached by cows as both they, sheep and walkers use them. In May and June enjoy the calls of the corncrakes.

Total Distance:	5½ miles/9km
Time:	3 hours
Maps:	OS Explorer 373/Landranger 48

30

Iona – south

Park and take the ferry as for walk 29.

The Abbey dates from the 13th century and is believed to have been built on the site of St Columba's 6th century monastery. From 1938 until 1965 extensive restoration has taken place. The Abbey and its surrounds are open to the public and in summer they are visited by many modern-day pilgrims. You will wish to stay for a long time in the quietness of the building and its cloisters. The Abbey community plays a vital part in the life of the island. Inside look for a huge slab of white marble, tinged with green, used as an altar table. It came from the quarry visited on this walk.

1 Walk ahead from the pier towards The Village (Baile Mor = big town!). Take the first left to pass the toilet block, a café and several shops. Stride the metalled road and follow it as it swings

Iona Abbey

uphill and inland for nearly a mile. At a cross of roads and tracks, walk left along a track past a white house. Beyond, the way deteriorates a little as it climbs to a gate, which gives access to the slopes. Follow the well-worn way to the ridge and then bear slightly left to walk on ahead, remaining on the high moorland. Below, there are glimpses of tiny sandy inlets. Follow the narrow path through a vast area of heather, beside a fence running ahead.

2 Where the fence turns right, stroll on for 400yds/370m towards the southern end of the island, keeping a close look out for a grassy gully that runs gently downwards towards the sea. At the foot of the gully you come to a grassy flat area, which is very wet but looks deceptively dry. On your right stand the foundations of two huts used by two marble quarry workers. Continue to the edge of the quarry, where you can see the machinery used until quarrying ended in 1914. As you drop gently down, look left to see a tiny reservoir of water used to provide power for the machinery. Notice the robust tanks, engine and cutting frame. Wander around to see other artefacts left just where they were being used, now coated with preservative to prevent further erosion. Beyond is a litter of blocks, cut ready for shaping. Clamber over these and look down to see the steep-sided outcrop against which a small boat, carrying coke

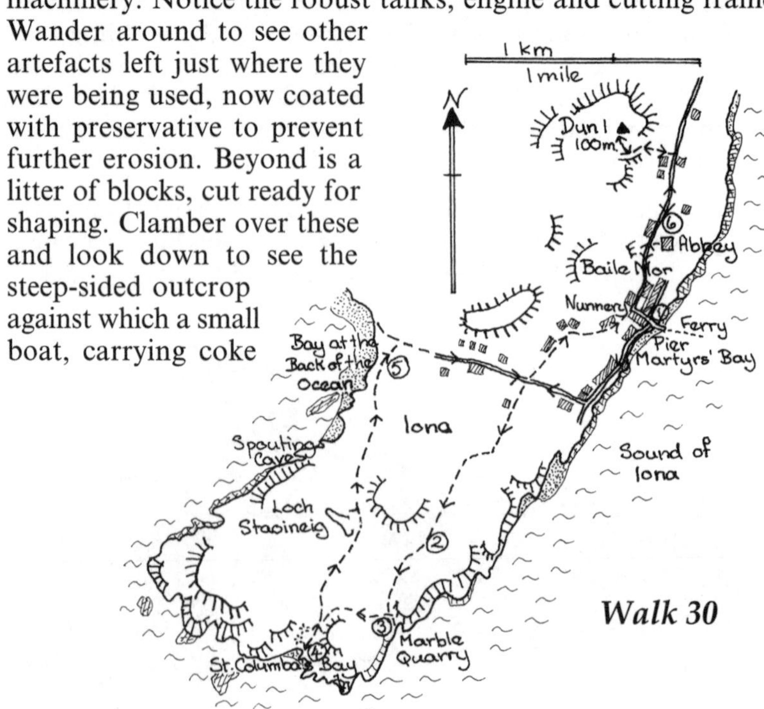

Oystercatchers

for the quarry's engine, would have unloaded. The dressed marble would have been taken away by the same boat.

3 Return to the ruined huts and swing left (west) picking the driest way, to continue to St Columba's Bay, where the saint and his disciples landed in 563 AD. This remote southern tip of the island is a very important place to Christians. Look for semi-precious stones, polished and rounded by the pounding of the sea.

4 From the beach walk inland along a path through a grassy valley, with high outcrops on either side. This sometimes muddy way, which is carried by low footbridges over the worst areas, brings you to the east side of Loch Staoineig, used as a reservoir. Follow the clear track, which soon begins to descend towards the magnificent, extensive machair that edges the Bay at the Back of the Ocean and is the site of Iona's golf course. This is a glorious vista of white shell-sand, bright green grass, and a turquoise sea, which soon shades to purple by seaweeds as the water deepens. Look left as you walk along the machair; if the tide is right and there is a rough sea you may see the plume from the blowhole of the Spouting Cave. You might also see curlews, oystercatchers and fulmars.

5 Stroll on until you reach the right branch of the track, which you take. Beyond the gate, a metalled road continues and brings you to the crossroads where you turned left at the start of the walk.

Turn left, this time, to return to The Village. Press on along the reinforced track, which is flanked with irises. Follow it to a gate onto a tarmacked road, where you turn right. Go past the next left turn to enter the 12th century nunnery, which is one of Scotland's most attractive ruins. Several gables stand tall. Leave by the gate in the far left corner and walk on to pass the heritage centre and the Iona's Church of Scotland, designed by Thomas Telford. On the roadside stands the medieval MacLean's Cross. Just before St Mary's Abbey is St Oran's Chapel and cemetery, where lie the bones of 60 kings, Scots, Irish, Norse and French. Duncan and Macbeth are both buried here and also, more recently, John Smith.

Yellow Iris

6 After visiting the Abbey continue along the road. Once past a white painted house on the left, pass through a well signposted stile and gate, on the left, onto a track. This leads towards the large mass of Dun I (pronounced Dun Ee) the highest hill on Iona. Follow the way where it swings left, and then climbs steadily to the summit cairn, 332ft/100m. From here you can see much of the island, a lovely sight. Return from the summit by your outward route.

Practicals

Type of walk: A delightful walk, with much to see. Wear strong footwear and carry suitable clothing in case the weather changes.

Total Distance:	7½ miles/12km
Time:	5–6 hours
Maps:	OS Explorer 373/Landranger 48

31a

A walk on Staffa

There are **boat trips** to Staffa from Oban, Tobermory, Iona and Ulva Ferry, with convenient parking nearby. As you go, look for seals basking on the skerries and for dolphins playing round the boat. You might also see whales and porpoises. As you approach the island, great rafts of puffins greet you, bouncing up and down on the waves.

The uninhabited island of **Staffa**, less than a mile long and about a third of a mile wide, lies seven miles off the west coast of Mull. Staffa's neighbouring islands are Gometra and Little Colonsay. Its famous landmark, Fingal's Cave, is inextricably linked with Mendelssohn's Overture 'The Hebrides'.

Fingal's Cave

Puffins

Hexagonal perpendicular basalt columns, set on a tufa base, rear up on either side of the yawning cavern. Above these columns, the columnar basalt lies horizontally. **The cave** is 228ft/69m long and 66ft/20m high. You are asked not to go beyond the barrier. Other huge caves, Boat, Great Face, Clamshell and Cormorant, pierce the dramatic cliffs.

1 If the sea is calm, you land at a concrete jetty by Clamshell Cave. From it, when the tide is on the ebb, you walk left over a natural causeway below the towering basalt, with a rope to assist you on the land side of the white-topped waves licking the hexagonal rocks to your left. This leads to the yawning entrance of Fingal's Cave where the booming of the pounding waves echoes deafeningly.

2 Return to the jetty and climb the strong ladder up onto Staffa's grassy top. Turn right and walk the narrow path over the sward. The way climbs several shallow hills and from these

Walk 31a

you have wonderful views to the Treshnish Isles, Tiree, Coll and Mull. Approach the cliffs quietly. In May and June, the puffins will allow you near their burrows. Pairs sit at the entrances and court, with much stroking of their large bills. Some are busy inside and pop out at the approach of a mate. Others return, extending their comical red legs and feet to make a perfect landing. Life is never dull in a puffin colony. Towards the far end, (north-east) steps drop down to a sheltered sea gully where landings can be attempted, when the swell is too strong for using the jetty.

3 Return along the narrow path over the flower-bedecked turf to walk to the opposite end of the island, near the top of the ladder. Go to the highest point, 105ft/32m from where you can see Iona and its Abbey. Then return down the ladder to the boat.

Practicals

Type of walk: Easy grassy walking, though since the sheep were removed in 1997 the vegetation has become taller and thicker, making the ground less easy to walk across. Any wet areas have duckboards. Take care near cliff edges when watching puffins. Concentrate as you walk along the roped causeway; some rocks can be slippery. Wear warm clothing and strong shoes. Carry a little food and water.

Total Distance:	2 miles/3.4km
Time:	As much time as allowed by the condition of the tide/sea
Maps:	OS Explorer 373/Landranger 48 (not needed)
NB:	Book the day before and check trip is on before setting off. Telephone Freephone 08000 85 87 86 for bookings and information. Information, and tickets, are also available at Tobermory T.I.C 01688 302182 or Craignure T.I.C 01680 812377

31b

Lunga, Treshnish Islands

Park as discussed in walk 31a.

Sea-girt Lunga, is the largest of the Tresnish Islands. In the year 2000 all the islands passed into the stewardship of The Hebridean Trust after receiving a grant from The Heritage Lottery Fund. The islands are formed from basaltic lavas that flowed from the volcano on Mull and, layer-upon-layer, once covered the seas around Mull. Treshnish, together with Staffa, are all that remains today of these once extensive plateau lavas.

Dutchman's Cap from Lunga

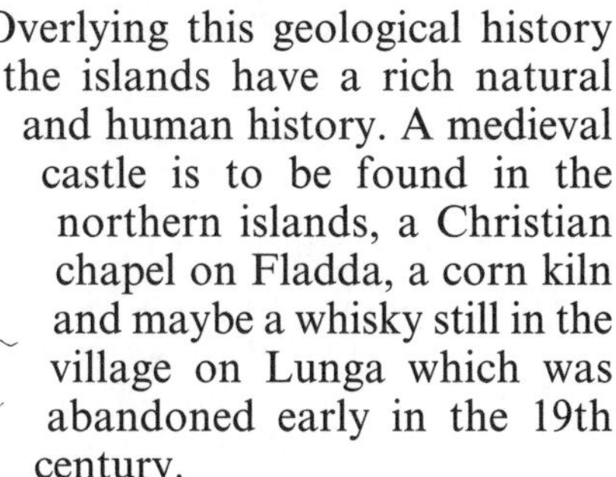

Walk 31b

Overlying this geological history the islands have a rich natural and human history. A medieval castle is to be found in the northern islands, a Christian chapel on Fladda, a corn kiln and maybe a whisky still in the village on Lunga which was abandoned early in the 19th century.

Landing on Lunga is by means of a floating jetty, which the boat collects and puts out to the shore. Walk up the cleared path through the boulders on the beach and turn left at the top to cross an area of low flat land, a raised beach. Listen for corncrakes as you go. Terns from the nearby skerries fly overhead but they are not nesting here so are not aggressive. It is quite an expensive trip but it is an unforgettable experience. For information about times etc, check with the T.I.C at Tobermory 01688 302182 or Craignure T.I.C 01680 812377.

1 Climb the twisting path through a rocky gully to another wave-cut platform at a higher level. Wind round to the right. Suddenly there are puffins everywhere, standing on the edge of the cliff, as interested in you as you are in them. The path continues along above the cliff; it winds round a deep geo, where there are razorbills and shags. Primroses, bluebells and thrift adorn the sheltered parts of the cliffs where there is deeper soil. Carry on along the path, which becomes narrower and more rocky, but is quite safe. Curve round another deep geo. Go past a fenced area where the path is very near to the cliff edge and then at a fork in the path take the right branch, going steeply downhill to another flat area. Opposite, across a deep cleft, is the Harp Rock, covered in guillemots. The noise (and smell) is unbelievable. On the near side of the cleft are

Razorbills

hundreds of puffins and razorbills, and shags nest under many of the large boulders, croaking at the intruders. You will want to spend some time here, taking in the amazing sight and sounds and being entranced by the fearless puffins.

2 When you can bear to tear yourself away or, when you need to be starting back for the boat, the quickest way is to retrace your steps. Or you can carry on round the flat platform, taking care where there are boulders in the grass. Gradually you leave the main concentration of birds behind. Quite a lot of Lunga still lies ahead but unless you spend less time watching the birds you are unlikely to be able to explore this. Instead head up a grassy slope to your left which will bring you to the highest point on the island. Continue along the ridge, enjoying the splendid views of the other islands and of Mull, then descend to the lower flatter ground at the north end of the ridge. If you look to your right you will find the remains of houses. Then carry on down bearing left to find the top of the gully path you came up. Go down and back across the flat low land to the beach and the boat.

Shag

Practicals

Type of walk: A must.

Total distance: As far as you wish
Time: 2 hours or however long you are allowed ashore
Maps: OS Explorer 374/Landranger 48

32

Salum and round Tiree's north-eastern coast

Park at grid ref 064478, on the side of the B8069, just after the road leaves Traigh Mhor (a huge sandy bay) and heads inland to Caolas, close to the north-east coast.

Tiree, the outermost of the Inner Hebrides, lies 20 miles/32km across the sea from Mull. It lies low on the edge of the Atlantic and is protected by the Gulf Stream. It is best known for being one of the sunniest places in Britain. It is also one of the windiest. Frost is rare and snow almost never falls. The island is very flat, but it has three hills, none higher that 460 feet/140m.

As you walk the sands at point 3 you might spot blue By-the-Wind Sailor (Velella),which looks like a small jellyfish, and Violet Sea Snail (Ianthina) washed up on the beach. They float in the plankton and are sometimes 'shipwrecked' after south-west gales. Velella has a sail and tentacles hanging down and Ianthina has a float of bubbles in mucus which it hangs from.

Crofthouses are to be found scattered throughout **Tiree**. There are few trees. Inland stretch single-track metalled roads, with marked passing places. These roads carry very little traffic and are a pleasure to walk. Indeed, nearly all of Tiree is grand for walking; there are few places you cannot go.

Blackhouse settlement, Brock

Walk 32

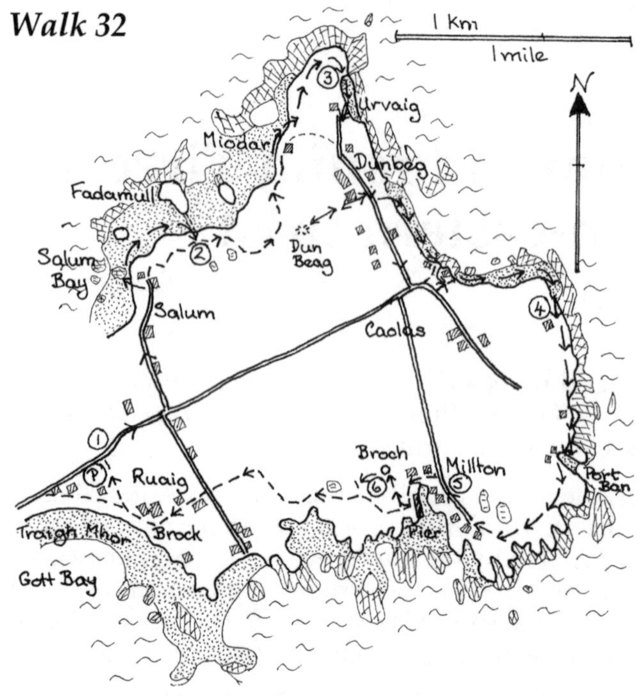

1 Walk on (east) from where you have parked to take the next left turn, signposted Salum. At the eastern end of Salum Bay, opposite the last farmhouse on the road, cross left to the shore. Here a tumble of boulders is all that remains of a massive causeway to An Dunan, a little fort on an isolated grass-covered rock. At high tide, water surrounds it. Go on, east, around the shoreline, where you might see dolphins disporting in the water and seals basking on a skerry. Half a mile from the dun look for the green Fadamull, once a tidal island, now connected to the shore by a ridge of boulders. Look for the remains of an ancient causeway that once provided the link.

2 At the end of the causeway go up onto a track which winds round behind the shore. The track swings inland and then out towards the shore again; just before the second bend, look right to see a green mound, Dun Beag, on the other side of a drainage ditch. Just before the farm, pass through a gate on the left, to continue along the sandy shore. Press on along the pleasant machair, keeping to the outside of a low stone wall. At the northernmost tip of

Tiree, where a mass of large boulders has been deposited by the tides, look across Gunna Sound to the island of Gunna and beyond to Coll.

Violet Sea Snail (Ianthina)

3 As you round the point, look south-east to see the Treshnish Isles, with the island, The Dutchman's Cap, standing bold. Beyond lies Mull. On reaching the dwelling of Urvaig, join a track that continues ahead. At the second cattle grid at the south end of the settlement of Dunbeg, walk, right, beside the fence on your left to a large green mound that lies up against a dyke you passed earlier. This is Dun Beag (large fort). Return to the road and walk on to the T-junction and turn left and then, almost immediately, right. Cross a cattle grid and bear left over the sandy turf to a stile over a fence. Then drop down the shallow cliffs to walk the glorious sands beside turquoise water. Here look for the By-the-Wind Sailor and the Violet Sea Snail. Alternatively, if you do not want to walk the road, take the signed track to the beach just after the cattle grid at the south end of Dunbeg. Then walk the delightful beach to the rocks at the far end. Go up to a fence corner behind a black-roofed house where a make-shift stile allows you to cross the fence easily. Walk behind the house and across the sandy turf to a stile.

4 Leave the pleasing bay by a typical Tiree house, built of local stone, the mortar being whitened and the stones left uncovered. Follow the fence beyond it down to the shore and go round the end of it on the rocks. Go on round the coast to pass a wooden house. Stroll on along low cliffs, striding over dwarf willow and heather, to pass a cottage at Port Ban. Follow one of several continuing sheep trods, keeping to rocky outcrops to avoid marshy troughs, to round the headland. Pass through a gap in a derelict wall and head for the rooftops and hydro-poles of Millton. Stride a large shingle ridge to go through a small gate, slightly right, through

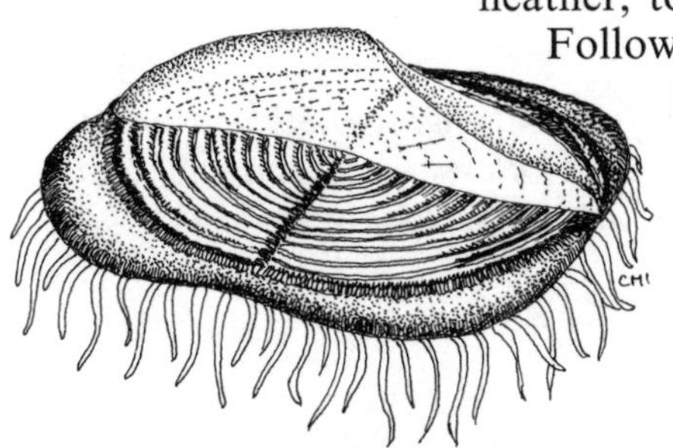

By-the-Wind Sailor (Velella)

the fence. Join a track by a renovated house, where an old black-house with five-feet thick walls has been incorporated into a pleasing dwelling. Follow the track through Millton, where you will see most of the few trees that grow on Tiree.

5 At a T-junction of tracks, bear left to walk past a small harbour used for lobster fishing. Pass through the gate and turn right to climb to the summit of the little hill (33yds/30m). A jumble of stones here is all that remains of a broch, Dun Mor a' Chaolais, a circular drystone fortified dwelling. Pause on the hillock to enjoy the spectacular view.

6 Descend from the hill to join a causeway track that bears right to run above wet ground. Pass through a gate, or take the stile over it at the bend in the track before the harbour, to walk a wide-fenced track. Cross a narrow road and continue on. Bear right towards the huge curving sandy bay, to pass the small settlement of Brock. Here a dozen or more blackhouses have been restored, with felted roof replacing thatch. Many other features have been retained. Walk across the links over a grassy track and, as you near a red-roofed bungalow, take the right branch to rejoin your car.

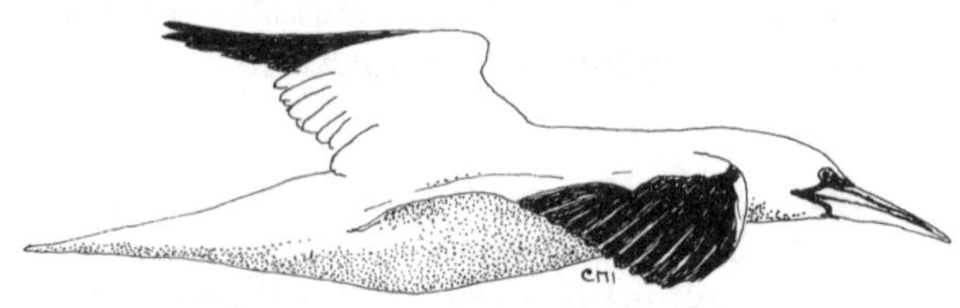

Gannet

Practicals

Type of walk: This is a delightful, challenging ramble around the north-eastern coast of Tiree. It follows tracks and pathless ways along the rocky coastline and takes you over glorious shell-sand bays.

Total Distance:	8 miles/13km
Time:	4–5 hours
Maps:	OS Explorer 372/Landranger 46

33

Vaul, Dun Mor Bhalla and the Ringing Stone, Tiree

Park on the west side of the post box on the B8069. This lies just before the left turn, off the B-road, to Vaul, grid ref 051473. To reach this, leave Scarinish by the B8068 and at Gott continue along the shoreside road (B8069).

The **bedrock of Tiree** is gneiss, but the creamiest of shell sand covers nearly all of the island. It is very flat and is 12 miles/19km long and varying in width from 1 mile/1.5km to 6 miles/10km. It is very fertile and it was once called The Granary of the Isles. Its Gaelic name Tir lodh translates as 'Land of corn'.

Dun Mor Bhalla is Tiree's most splendid broch. Climb into the circular drystone base of the one-time tower, which would have

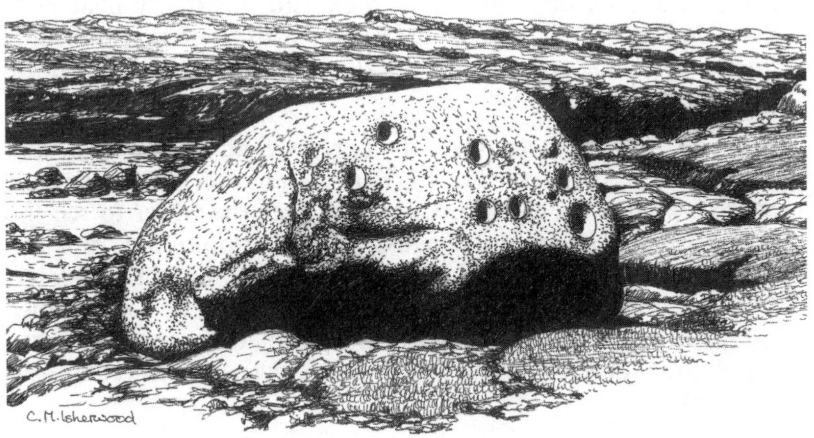

The Ringing Stone

Walk 33

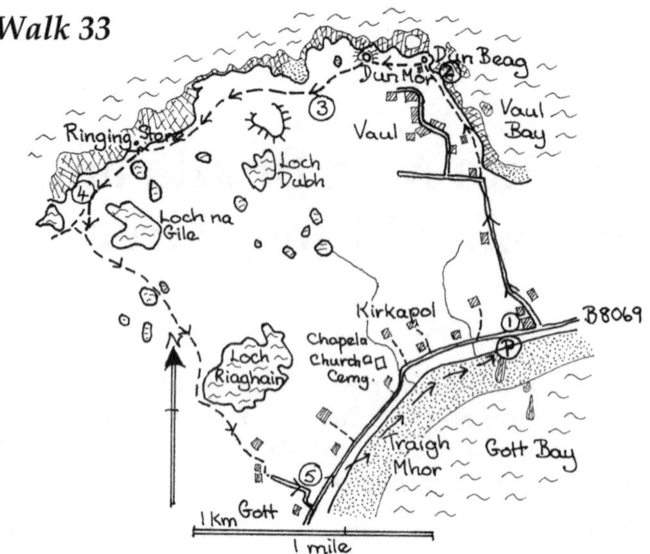

been a fortified home. Look for the steps and gallery. Outside you can trace a perimeter wall, perhaps where cattle were coralled, or the family lived, moving into the tower in times of trouble.

The Ringing Stone, Clach a'Choire, is believed to be an erratic, a stone deposited by a glacier far from its origin, in this case Rum. It stands on a plinth of rock and has many neat cup-shaped hollows in it. Strike the boulder with a pebble and hear it ring. Legend says that if the erratic is shattered, Tiree will be overwhelmed by the sea.

1 From the parking area, walk the narrow road in the signposted direction for the township of Vaul. Continue beside the golf course, where sheep graze. Look out over the water to see the Cuillin of Skye peeping through a gap in the mountains of Rum. To the right, with its distinctive cliffs, lies Eigg and to the left of Rum you can just discern the Uists. Where the road swings left, continue ahead along the shore and then bear left onto the shallow cliffs, from where you might spot seals, eider and shelduck.

2 Continue round Vaul Bay to climb a steep-sided grassy hill, Dun Beag, an Iron-Age fort, once impregnable from the sea. From the

Shelduck

top you can see the island of Barra. Go on to climb a stile over a fence where there is an interpretive board and continue on to visit, high on its grassy hill, Dun Mor Bhalla. Return down the little path and walk on through vast outcrops of gneiss. Pass Loch an Fhaing, on your right.

3 Climb the stile over the fence and go on round the sandy bay. Continue on along the cliffs of gneiss, taking care as you round several sheer-sided ravines which pierce the way. Follow the narrow path over a grassy sward and then pass, on the left, a wet area with small pools. As Loch Dubh a'Gharraidh Fail comes into view, look behind the shore rocks and across a sandy area from the path, to see the strange large grey formless boulder, the Ringing Stone, which you will want to visit. Then press on along the shoreline until you reach a waymarked gate through a fence.

4 Here, don't pass through. Turn left before the gate to go along the outer edge of the fence until you reach a clear track going inland. Turn left and follow it. It is a delight to walk and brings you close to Loch na Gile, a place for some bird watching. Head on through a very wet area where you will appreciate the sturdy track, and then pass between two lochans. Go through a derelict gate by stepping over it at the lowest place and walk on, keeping to the right of Loch Riaghain, where you might spot whooper swans. Stroll on to join the narrow road at Gott farm, where you turn left and continue to the B8069.

5 Turn left and walk towards the hotel. Turn left before it, to visit two ancient stone chapels. The chapel within the burial ground probably dates from the 14th century. The ruined chapel behind, standing alone on a hillock, is thought to be even older. Spend time looking at the gravestones, some of which are very old. Return to the huge curving sands of Traigh Mhor (Gott Bay), and then, before returning to where you have parked, you might still have time to watch the wind surfers and kite surfers (if present). Their level of skill is amazing.

Greylag geese

Practicals	
Type of walk: There is something of interest around each corner. Generally easy walking along narrow paths. Can be wet in places. Steep scramble up to the duns.	
Total Distance:	6 miles/9.5km
Time:	3 hours
Maps:	OS Explorer 372/Landranger 46

34

Hynish, Happy Valley and Dun na Cleite, Tiree

Park in the car park before the pier, grid ref 986393. To reach this follow the signs directing you round on a track. To reach Hynish take the B8065 from Scarinish until you can turn left onto the B8066 to carry on.

Skerryvore Lighthouse is a legend of Victorian building endeavour. It is well worthwhile to spend time visiting the Signalling Tower Museum, where the displays dramatically show how, over a period of five years, great stone blocks were shipped to Tiree and shaped to the exact size needed to complete the massive edifice.

1 To reach Happy Valley, as the hidden hollow is known, continue to the end of the road. Stride along the continuing track to pass through a series of gates (please close). Cross in front of Millport House and climb the stile by a gate opposite, to reach the grassland at the back of the shore. Here join a track which helps you avoid the worst of the wet, then wind right round a rocky hill. Go on to negotiate a marshy area to reach the long grassy valley, (Happy Valley), which is flanked by towering gneiss. The lonely vale slopes gently towards the sea. Beyond a huge wall of pebbles lies a delightful sandy bay.

2 Wind round left at the far end of the beach and cross a small grass and

Signalling Tower, Hynish

rock headland down onto the pebbles. Here are several fantastic small natural arches and wave-sculpted rocks, which are fun to explore. Look for fulmars and kittiwakes.

3 Dun na Cleite stands high on the left at the opposite end of the bay. Walk round the lower part of the hill; then an easy way to ascend is seen. The remains of two small walls, almost obscured by sand and vegetation, are all that is visible of the fort. Pause to enjoy the view of Skerryvore Lighthouse, then make your way carefully down the far side of the dun, zigzagging down natural ramps. Walk round the seaward side of the next hill and up a valley, which becomes more of a groove at the top, to join your outward route. Or you could return exactly by your outward route.

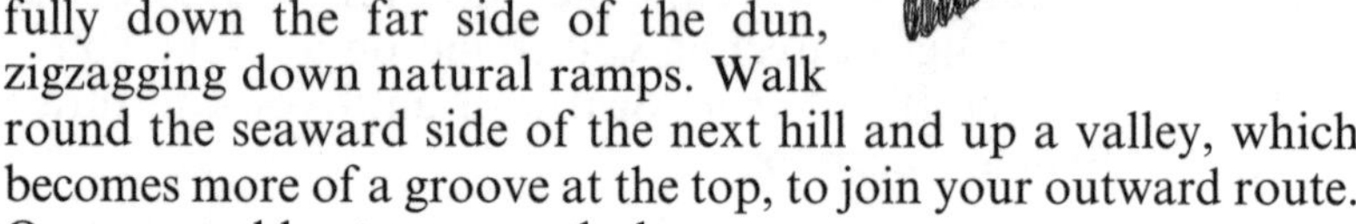

Fulmar

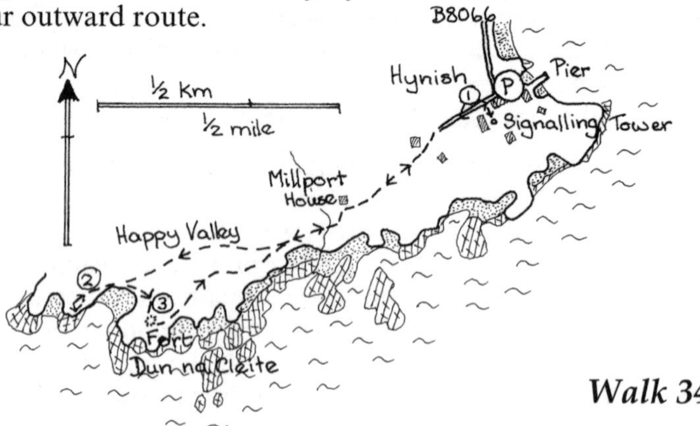

Walk 34

Practicals

Type of walk: Easy walking except for the marshy area. The cliffs on the sea side are sheer and, on the climb to the dun, therefore children should be under control.

Total Distance:	2 miles/3.5km
Time:	An afternoon
Maps:	OS Explorer372/Landranger 46

35

Kenavara, Tiree

Park on the verge, grid ref 945426, where the continuation of the B8065 turns sharply right towards Sandaig. To reach this, take the B8065 west from Scarinish and follow it to its end. Then continue ahead where it becomes a minor road for a short way to the sharp bend and the parking verge.

As you drive, cycle or walk through the island you cross a totally flat area known as The Reef. Therefore **Kenavara** presents a great surprise. It is a rugged, precipitous and deeply riven pink gneiss headland, some 300ft/92m in height.

Loch a'Phuill is the largest stretch of fresh water on Tiree. It is shallow, just behind the beach, surrounded by machair and so is very attractive to birds. There are large flocks of duck and whooper swans in winter, and along the edges you might spot many waders, notably black-tailed godwit.

1 Pass through a kissing gate beside the field gate, and follow the sign 'to the beach'. Stride ahead over the sandy way. Look out for golden plovers running over the turf. Follow the route through the pale dunes to pass through another kissing gate.

Ceann a'Mhara (Kenavara)

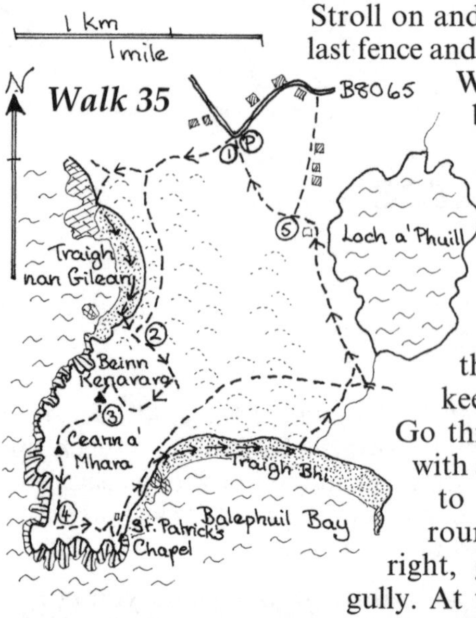

Stroll on and go through the gate in the last fence and bear left down to the beach. Walk round the lovely sandy bay to the far end, below the dramatic bulk of Kenavara (Ceann a'Mhara) and go through a kissing gate with a sign 'to Teampuill Pharaig'.

2 Begin the steep climb up the north side of Kenavara, keeping the fence to your left. Go through another kissing gate with a similar sign, but turn right to follow the fence up and round. When the fence turns right, go with it into a narrow gully. At the top climb left out of it (quite shallow now) to reach the cairn on top of Mullach Mor. Wander around this glorious top. Enjoy the wild flowers and the catkin-laden dwarf willow. Look out to sea, where Skerryvore lighthouse stands like a tall thin pencil. Overhead fulmars and kittiwakes fly to their nests on the many ledges of the cliffs. Look inland to see the large shallow sandy Loch a'Phuill and, to its south, the magnificent curve of the seashore, Traigh Bhi.

3 As you leave the summit wind slightly left, then pick up the old wall that soon joins a new fence. This runs down the shoulder and then up again towards the southerly headland. Just as you begin to climb, look seaward along a long rocky promontory. Close to its natural cairn, an upstanding sturdy tussockof grass created by erosion, is the site of a dun, one of several thought to have been constructed on Kenavara. Go on to the splendid old cairn covered with lichens, on the second summit, Kenavara. Continue around the delightful headland. Here, more fulmars nest among dark pink campion, scurvy grass and primrose. Lower down on some dark, damp ledges shags sit on their untidy nests.

Creeping Willow

4 Follow the fence to its end, walking above some fine rock stacks and clefts. Then bear left and contour across the hillside, picking your way round outcrops, until you can drop down to the seaward end of Balephuill Bay and join a clear path past the ruins of St Patrick's Chapel, with its two cross stones. Then follow the narrow path to the start of Traigh Bhi. Notice the many low stone walls, enclosing oblong areas, once used for drying kelp. When you can bear to leave the lovely bay, walk along the sand to the outflow of the burn and turn, left, into the dunes on a good track. Do not cross the cattle grid or the bridge over the burn, but bear left continuing on the track that runs parallel with the west shore of the Loch a'Phuill, seen from the top of Kenavara. This is a wonderful place for bird watching.

5 Carry on along the on-going path, which soon develops into a grassy track across the machair. Then keep beside the fence to go through a gate. Beyond, carry on along the good track, with the fence to your right, until you reach the gate and kissing gate beside your car.

Golden Plover

Practicals

Type of walk: This ramble explores Kenavara, a rugged, precipitous and deeply riven pink gneiss headland some 300ft/90m in height, which lies to the south west of Tiree. Generally easy walking. Steep climb all the way up to the summit. Take care on the cliffs. Shut all gates and close securely.

Total Distance:	6 miles/9.5km
Time:	3–4 hours
Maps:	OS Explorer 372/Landranger 46

36

Beinn Hough, Tiree

Park at Sandaig, grid ref 940437. To reach this leave Scarinish by the B8065 and at its end, continue on ahead on the minor road to Sandaig.

Before setting off on your walk, visit the fascinating **Sandaig Musuem**, where a historic crofter's cottage, complete with byre and barn has been restored. Inside you can see the type of furniture used and the layout of the rooms. Entry is free and the museum is staffed by volunteers and managed by The Hebridean Trust. Open Monday to Friday 2pm–4pm from Easter to late September.

Visit the **ancient chapel of St Kenneth**, a friend of St Columba. The roofless ruin lies in the sand dunes, each stone heavily encrusted with golden lichen. Early in this century a small bronze bell was found in the remains.

1 Proceed north along the narrow road, cross a cattle grid and continue on to pass two gates on the left, opposite a house. Go on along the road to a third gate, on the left, where there is an interpretive board. You can see the chapel wall from here. Walk over to it.

Museum, Sandaig

Walk 36

2 Return to the gate and stroll on along the road to cross the cattle grid. Bear left and, very soon, right, along the road that climbs round the seaward side of Cnoc an Fhithich, where there are two tall telecommunication masts. As you ascend you can see Skerryvore lighthouse, Barra and the Uists. From the road up the hill, look left down a sloping sward, where a mass of deep purple marsh orchids flowers. Below, on wide grassy links, cattle graze about Loch Earblaig. At the first mast Loch a'Phuill and Kenavara come into view. Bear left to climb to the next mast on the hill and then continue along the airy way, with the sea to the left. Jura and Islay lie on the horizon.

3 Drop down with care to a grassy glen and then ascend to the trig point on Beinn Hough, 388ft/127m. Pause here to enjoy the island spread out before you, flat, green, with deep blue lochs and golden curving bays – and the 'golf ball' on Beinn Hynish. From this high point you can see the many cattle and sheep, and crofters at work on their rolling land. Then start your descent by some concrete steps, which are edged with concrete posts, and when these swing right, go on climbing down steadily to the sandy links. Walk on to join a track and bear left. Follow the reinforced way to Traigh Hough and stroll left along the sands, or the pebbles of a huge bank if the tide is in. Or you can continue

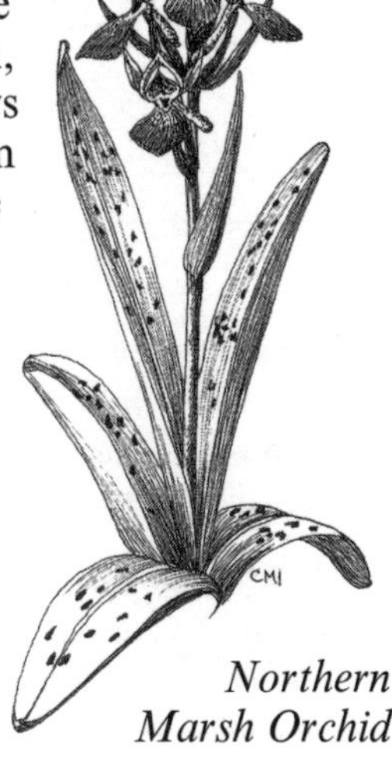

Northern Marsh Orchid

behind the marram, where there are many paths, to the end. As you go look for pied wagtails, dunlin, sanderlings, turnstones and ringed plover. You might also see seals bobbing up from the deep-blue water.

4 Continue over the dunes, where there are many rows of small boulders once used for drying seaweed for kelp. Walk round the small bay of Traigh Thallasgair, and then a bay full of pebbles. Go through a gate in the fence. Head on to Dun Hanais, a galleried dun. Then carry on down to a kissing gate, which gives access to the next beach, Traigh Thodhrasdail, with its great wall of creamy sand dunes, which lies below Kilkenneth. Towards the end of the beach, a large exposure of granite glows bright pink. Climb up onto the shallow dunes above Traigh Ghrianal and saunter on, outside the fence. Pass through a gate and walk on to step across Abhainn na Cille and then begin to strike over the extensive greensward towards the road where you will see some of the many lapwings that frequent Tiree. Turn right to rejoin your car.

Ringed plovers and dunlin

Practicals

Type of walk: Generally easy walking but best wear stout shoes or boots. Choose a good day to enjoy the spectacular views and the lovely beaches. If it's very windy standing might be a problem.

Total Distance:	4½ miles/7.5km
Time:	2–3 hours
Maps:	OS Explorer 372/Landranger 46

West Coast and Calgary Point, Coll

Park on the sandy sward, grid ref 152538, beyond the cattle grid, at the end of the B8070. To reach this, continue to The Roundhouse. Park here to view the two castles. Then continue on to the end.

Coll is an island of rock, heather, green pastures and sand dunes. It is edged with glorious silver-sand bays that are hemmed by cliffs, crags and whale-backs of gneiss. Most of the population live in the village of Arinagour at the head of Loch Eatharna. It is an attractive village, with a row of white-washed cottages provided in the 19th century by Alexander MacLean, the laird, for the workers on his estate. The name Arinagour means 'shelter of the goats'.

There are two **Breachacha Castles**. The 'Old Castle', nearer the shore, is white and magnificent and dates from the 15th century. In 1961 it was bought by Major Nicholas MacLean Bristol, a descendant of the MacLeans of Coll, who has restored it. The

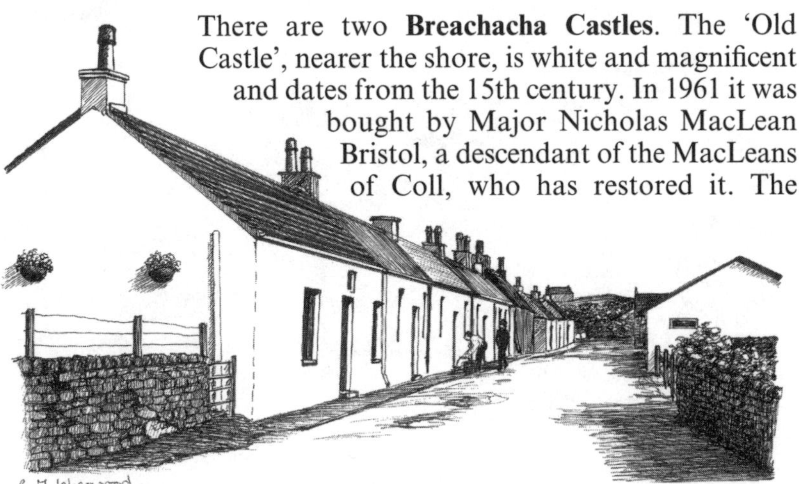

Arinagour

'New Castle', 18th century and dramatically turreted, was built for the chief of the Coll MacLeans. Here Dr Johnson and Boswell stayed. To view the two Breachacha Castles from over pastures, turn left at the dwelling curiously named The Roundhouse. (This is thought to be the site of a round watch-tower for the original castle, but the tower was later replaced by the house.) Continue along the narrow road to view them and then return to The Roundhouse.

1 Turn left and go on to the end of the road to park on the sandy sward. Walk left (south) along the continuing sandy track to reach the mile-long stretch of golden sands, Traigh Chrossapol. Turn left and stroll a short way, then negotiate a fence soon after you leave the bay, to stroll inland, heading for MacLean's Tomb. This is a dilapidated stone building, with twin turrets, guarding an arched doorway into the walled, roofless, square enclosure. It was built in 1805 by Alexander MacLean for his wife, and he also was interred later.

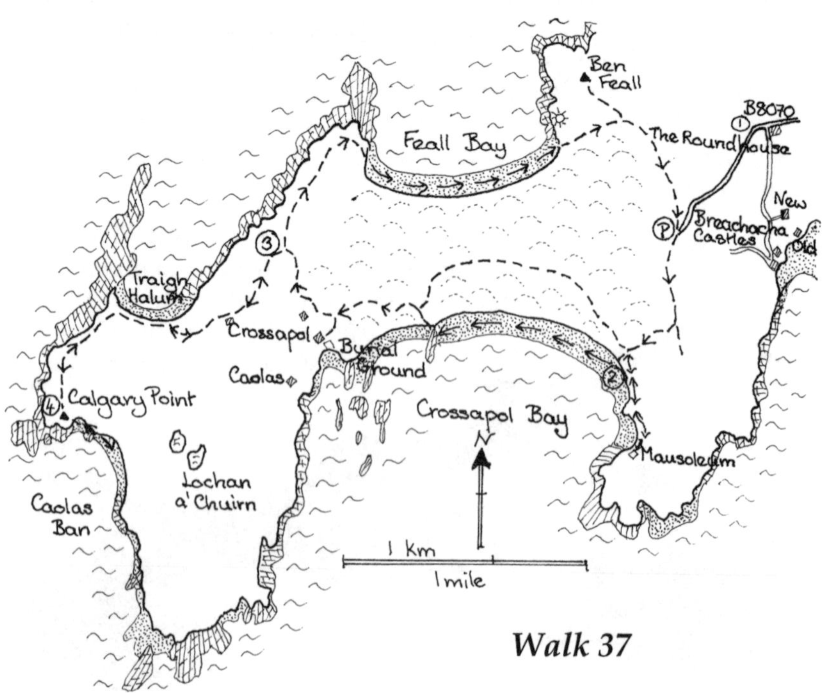

Walk 37

Sanderling

2 Return to the shore and head west along the glorious bay. Ahead ringed plovers race over the sand and on the green sward dunlin feed. Just beyond the rocky outcrop in the middle of the bay, go up into the sand dunes to pass through a small gate to reach a sign 'Calgary Point 2¾ miles/4.5km'. Turn left and wind down into a hollow to join a grassy track, heading for Crossapol House. There are waymarks at intervals and as you near the house you come to another signpost. Walk ahead in the direction indicated for Calgary Point. Go through the dunes, then keep the fence to your left. Ahead is a waymarked post on a hillock; pick up a grassy track, which leads past it. Then go downhill towards a gate, passing through a gap to the left of it. Follow the fence to a three-armed signpost.

3 Turn left for Calgary Point and follow the sparse waymarks over the moor to cross a fence at a stile and go uphill towards a shed. Look and listen for lapwings feeding in the long grass. From here go down to a lovely curving bay and walk along behind it through the marram. Eiders and red-throated divers fish in the sheltered water. The waymarks continue behind the shore. Eventually you come to a gate and beyond it, Calgary Point, where there is a trig point and splendid views across to Gunna and Tiree. Go on to the next bay, which is delightful and a lovely place for a pause and perhaps a picnic. Look for sanderlings running along the tideline and turnstones on the rocks.

4 Retrace your steps to the three-armed signpost. From here walk ahead following the sign for Feall Bay, across pleasant short flowery turf, with cliffs away to the left. this is a delightful part of the walk. Curve round to the right and go uphill to cross a low ridge, with reefs and islets out to the left and then wind down towards Feall Bay, the 'bay of betrayal'. Go through a small wooden gate and descend to the sands. If you still have lots of energy left you might like to climb Ben Feall, the 'hill of betrayal' Coll's second highest hill. It is difficult to believe that in this delightful corner of the island dastardly deeds occurred in the past. There is a path that goes left just about at the point where the other track turns right. Come down the same way and stroll down the main track to the car.

Lapwing

Practicals

Type of walk: This is a glorious walk taking you to some fine sands. Easy walking all the way.

Total Distance: 8½ miles/13.5km
Time: 5–6 hours
Maps: Os Explorer 372/Landranger 46

38

Totronald, Coll

Park in the small car park, grid ref 168562, provided by the RSPB. To reach this leave Arinagour by the B8070. At the T-junction at Arileod turn right and drive on to the end of the road.

The **turnstone** does not breed in this country even though it is present at all seasons. It is known as a passage migrant, as a winter visitor, and many stay along our shores all summer. It is a wader of the rocky shore, though on sandy shores it is often seen hunting along the seaweed at the tide edge. It is a short-legged bird with orange legs and a short slightly up-tilted bill, which it uses like a pick-axe to lever up and tip over a stone. It then quickly pounces on sand hoppers, small crabs and molluscs below.

1 Walk back from the car park, slightly uphill, to see two standing stones known as 'the Tellers of Tales' in a pasture on the left. Here also is the visitor centre, which has an interesting display. Just by the car park stands the corncrake viewing platform with a seat and a good view over the adjacent fields.

Clach na Ban-righ, Ben Hogh

Walk 38

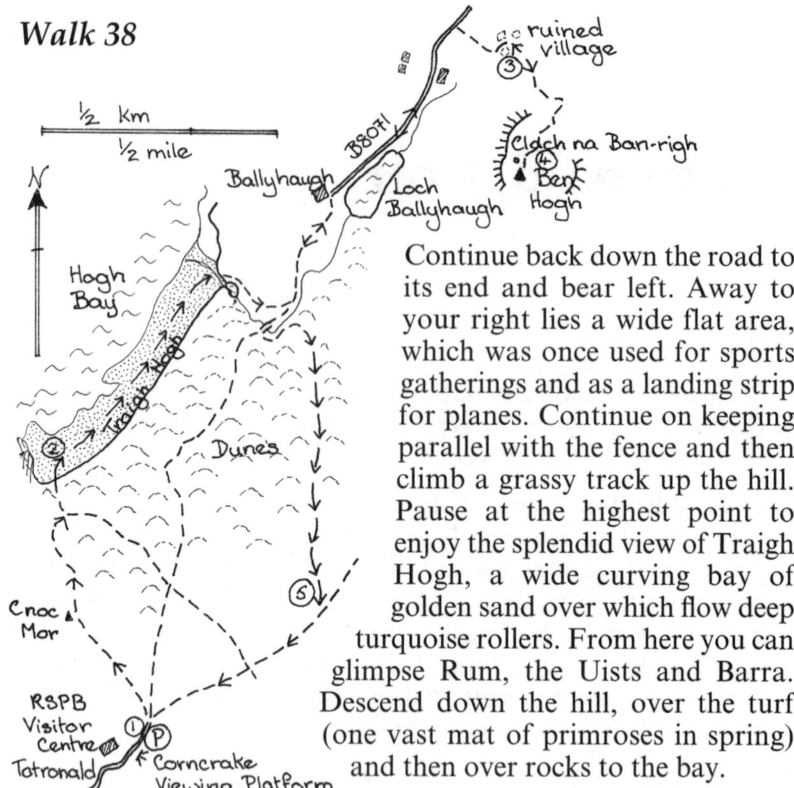

Continue back down the road to its end and bear left. Away to your right lies a wide flat area, which was once used for sports gatherings and as a landing strip for planes. Continue on keeping parallel with the fence and then climb a grassy track up the hill. Pause at the highest point to enjoy the splendid view of Traigh Hogh, a wide curving bay of golden sand over which flow deep turquoise rollers. From here you can glimpse Rum, the Uists and Barra. Descend down the hill, over the turf (one vast mat of primroses in spring) and then over rocks to the bay.

2 Walk north east along the shore where to your right tower dunes 50ft/15m high. Here look for sanderling, ringed plover, oystercatchers and turnstones. At the end of the bay, step across the burn, which flows out of Loch Ballyhaugh, and follow it upstream to the track through the dunes. Pass through a gate on the left. Stride the track ahead, keeping right of Ballyhaugh, the Hebridean Centre for the Project Trust, which places volunteeers overseas. Pass through another gate to join a narrow road. Carry on ahead beside the pleasing Loch Ballyhaugh, where a pair of mute swans nest. Continue on to cross a cattle

Turnstone

grid. Above, on the left, are two thatched cottages. Stroll on to pass through, on the right, a gate that gives access to a track leading to a ruined croft. Behind stand several more ruins.

3 From the first ruin, follow the path ahead to a gap in the stone wall, and make your way over a broken stile between two gate stoops. Go ahead up a shallow gully to the ridge and then wind up the ridge along a small path to the summit of Ben Hogh, 339ft/112m, and a perched boulder named Clach na Ban-righ (the Queen's Stone). It is perched on three small rocks, left there by a retreating ice flow. From the trig point there is a wonderful view of the three hills on Tiree, the island of Gunna between Tiree and Coll, Skerryvore lighthouse, Eigg, Rum, the Cuillin on Skye, Barra, and the Uists. Further to the east, Ben Nevis and Ben More can be seen.

4 Return down the hill and turn left to walk past the loch and the Centre. Carry on along the track and pass through a gate. Keep on the track until you have crossed the burn on a bridge, then turn left through a hollow and curve left up a path. Climb the dunes and wind right along the high ground, remaining parallel with the fence and gradually converging with it. Follow the fence as it bears south. Here, the dunes are pitted with rabbit holes and the occupants sunbathe on grassy slopes. Look for dog lichen growing among the grass and a tiny pink cranesbill.

Dog lichen

5 When Totronald comes into view, head in that direction, descending to the flat sandy area and join a track here. Go on ahead to join the road at the car park.

Practicals

Type of walk: A very pleasant walk across pasture, along a dramatic shore, beside a loch before climbing up a fine little hill with a great view.

Total Distance:	6 miles/9.5km
Time:	3 hours
Maps:	OS Explorer 372/Landranger 46

39

Cornaigbeg, Coll and Beart an Fhir

Park just before a cattle grid, grid ref 234628. To access this, leave Arinagour by the B8071. At the crossroads, turn right onto the B8072 and continue for 2½ miles/4km.

As you drive along the **B8072** to start your walk, you pass Cranaig. The road beyond was not metalled until the 1920s. Then you pass Gallanach, where in the 1950s and 60s tulips and daffodils were exported from the island. After driving up Windy Gap, you descend to pass Killunaig Chapel and graveyard, which you might like to visit. Towards the end of the first part of your walk, on returning to the road, you might wish to make a short diversion. Turn left and walk on to take a track, going off right. This leads to **Bousd**, once a busy township, with over a hundred people, a school and a church. Ten years ago two or three of the ruined houses had been restored. If you walked up either the left or right branch of the track you could see the sad remains of more ruined houses. Today, happily, more of the cottages have been restored.

Ruined croft, Bousd

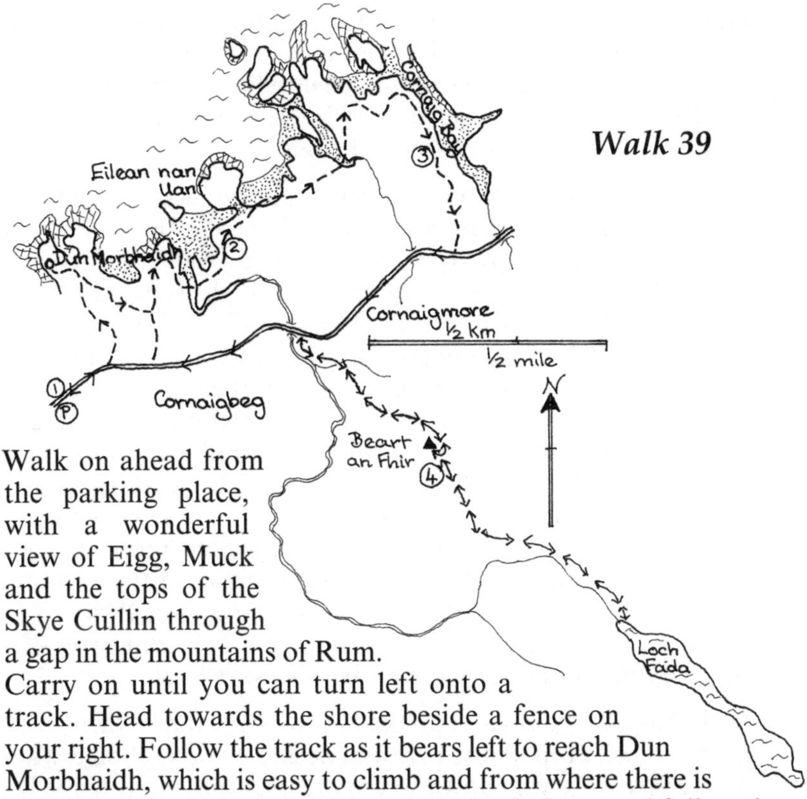

Eilean nan Uan
Dun Morbhaidh
Cornaig Bay
Cornaigmore
Cornaigbeg
Beart an Fhir
Loch Faida
½ Km
½ mile
N

Walk 39

1 Walk on ahead from the parking place, with a wonderful view of Eigg, Muck and the tops of the Skye Cuillin through a gap in the mountains of Rum. Carry on until you can turn left onto a track. Head towards the shore beside a fence on your right. Follow the track as it bears left to reach Dun Morbhaidh, which is easy to climb and from where there is a fine view along the coast. Then come back down and follow the grassy track along the edge of the field above the sandy bay, go past a caravan and on to a corner where the track turns right. Here go through a gate into the rough field beyond and follow the fence along above the bay. Go through a gully in the rocks and come down grassy slopes to a wide shallow burn, which you can ford easily at all but the highest tides.

Grey seal

2 Wind round the next fence on the rocks, well above high tide level. From here you might spot seals, otters and turnstones. (If the tide is out you might wish to visit the lovely green island, Eilean nan Uan). Follow the contours around the seaward side of the next area of high dunes, from where there is a glorious view ahead. Go on along the deeply indented coastline, which has innumerable sandy pockets. Step across another stream and press on over great outcrops of gneiss until you come to the side of Cornaig Bay. Walk, right, along its shoreline. In the latter years of the 19th century, the bay was very busy, being used by east-coast fishermen for several months of the year.

3 Soon a fence appears on your left, and you need to wind right round an outcrop. Then go uphill and keep to the high ground, which is generally grassy and pleasant to walk, until you can come down easily to where the fence meets the road. Go through a gate and if you wish to visit Bousd, walk left, otherwise turn right and walk on downhill on the 'dual carriageway'. Before the burn at the foot of the hill, walk left over the grass to a gate with a kissing gate beside it. Pass through and climb the hill beside the electricity poles. Cross a small burn and climb the rocky hillocks beyond, to follow the high ground towards Beart an Fhir, the highest hill in the vicinity, which appears as a great rock bastion from this angle. Keep to its left side where there is a gully between rock walls. Go up this until a break in the cliff above allows you to climb easily to a col. The summit of Beart an Fhir is on your right and from it you have a splendid view of the heathery moorland stretching towards Loch Fada.

4 Walk back to the col and up the next lower summit, then cross to another rocky top. Pause here and decide if you wish to continue. You can see the way down to the loch, a long grassy slope bearing right to a fence corner where there is a kissing gate. Then a long boggy valley leads to the loch. Alas the way can be even wetter if you wish to walk round the loch so pausing on the hill before returning by your outward route might be the best option. At the road turn left to return to the parking area.

Practicals

Type of walk: This is an interesting walk. The way along the shore contrasts greatly with the walk over moorland to view the loch from on high.

Total Distance:	4 miles/6.5km
Time:	3 hours
Maps:	OS Explorer 372/Landranger 46

40a

Struan Rubha Mor

Park on a wide grass verge by the gate with a footpath sign to Struan Rubha Mor, grid ref 254637. To access this, drive north-west along the B8071 from Arinagour, and at the T-junction turn right onto the B8072. Drive past Cornaigbeg and the 'dual carriageway', until you see the footpath sign on your left.

Storm petrels spend most of their lives out on the open ocean in spite of their small size. They feed on plankton picked off the surface of the water. It is said that the name petrel comes from St Peter walking on the water. They come ashore to nest in crevices in rocks, walls and even under large pebbles at the top of the beach. Both they and the shearwaters only come back to their nests at night to feed their young in order to avoid predators such as gulls and skuas.

1 Go through the gate and follow the sandy track across the field.

Traigh Bhousd

Walk 40a

It soon becomes grassy and curves round to descend through dunes to Traigh Bhousd, a fine sandy bay curving to a tidal islet in the middle, where you will want to pause or explore.

2 Return up the track and turn off right through a gate, with a sign to Rubha Mor, into another field, which is full of silverweed. Wind right, following an indistinct track, which becomes much clearer beyond a low ridge. Cross a boggy area with a ditch and walk ahead through a valley between rocky walls. Towards the end of the valley the path takes to the right side and climbs gently; it is now a broad, grassy way with a retaining wall on the left. It curves round a valley and climbs again, and then suddenly stops. An ordinary path goes on. There are four concrete plinths near the abrupt end of the made track; probably for gun emplacements during the 1939–45 war.

3 Carry on along the crest of the ridge towards the sea and stop when you reach the end! This is a wonderful place to sit and watch the waves pounding in to smash in a welter of foam on the rocks below. Out at sea gannets dive for fish and auks and kittiwakes fly past. At the right time of year, and with a westerly wind blowing, you may see Manx shearwaters and storm petrels quite close in shore.

Storm Petrel

4 Return by your outward route.

Practicals

Type of walk: A lovely exhilarating short walk.

Total Distance:	1 mile/1.5km
Time:	1 hour
Maps:	OS Explorer 372/Landranger 46

Sorisdale and the North beach

Park on the wide verge, taking care not to obstruct any gateways, grid ref 269633. To access this see walk 40a and then drive to the end of the road at Sorisdale. Turn in the designated turning place and drive 55yds/50m back up the road to park on the verge.

Sorisdale has many ruins and was for a long time just a single croft. Today many of the houses have been rebuilt and the land around is farmed. There are both cattle and sheep and, also, greylag geese in the fields. During excavation at Sorisdale, the shelter and skeletal remains of a 'Beaker person', who lived on Coll about 2000BC, were revealed.

1 Walk back down the road and through the gate, where a sign says 'private road' and another indicates footpaths to two bays. Walk ahead past a cottage to a left turn and a notice to 'beach', with an arrow left and one straight ahead. Go on ahead, but

North Beach (Traigh Tuath)

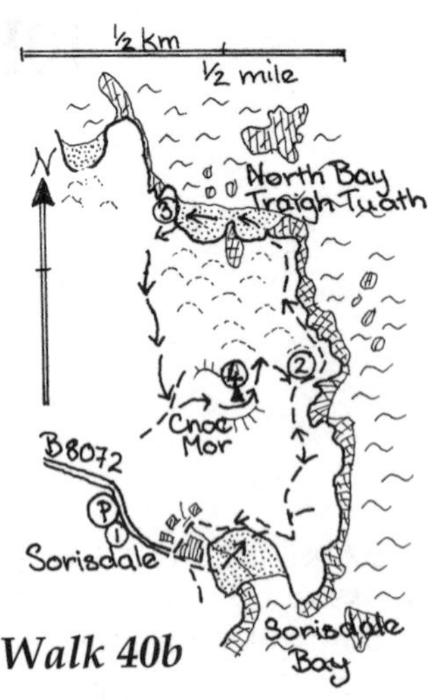

Walk 40b

almost immediately leave the track and walk down a grassy way to the lovely sandy bay of Sorisdale. You may find ringed plovers running over the sand and an offshore islet covered with cormorants. Walk left along the sand in front of another cottage, and go up the grass at the far side to join a sandy track. Follow this round a bend, but at the next bend, where it goes right, leave it and go along beside a fence round the left side of a hillock. Carry on down a clear path to a corner. Cross a burn on a wooden bridge and continue along the fence to pass through a gate.

2 Go across the field beyond and wind right to contour above the shore. There is a good clear path through the marram just above the rocky inlet and bays. Enjoy the stunning views north to the offshore islands with Rum and Eigg behind. Come round a corner and then descend gently to a beautiful sandy bay, Traigh Tuath (North Bay), divided by a rocky spit, where you might wish to pause. Here common seals come close inshore, and kittiwakes, shags and cormorants frequent the rocks offshore.

3 Leave the beach by the far corner and make your way up through the marram and across the machair, in September bright with grass of Parnassus, eyebright, thyme, wild carrot and clover. Head for the high ground, a low hill called Cnoc Mor, south of the bay. Go along a rib of rocky hummocks then cross an indistinct track and climb the steep grass beyond outcrops of rock to reach the first top of Cnoc Mor. Then walk round its delightful grassy craggy ridge to the summit. The view is spectacular, north to Canna, Rum and Eigg with Muck in front of it, then across to Ardnamurchan and Mull and south over Coll. On a clear day you can see the Outer Isles.

Kittiwake

4 Descend east by a grassy ridge, heading towards the field corner. Curve left, using animal paths to leave the ridge when the way becomes rougher. Then wind round right again to come down by the fence. Go through the gate and follow your outward route back as far as Sorisdale Bay. Here keep on the track through the cottages, crossing a burn on a wooden footbridge, to turn right at the main track. Go through the gate and walk up the road to the parking area.

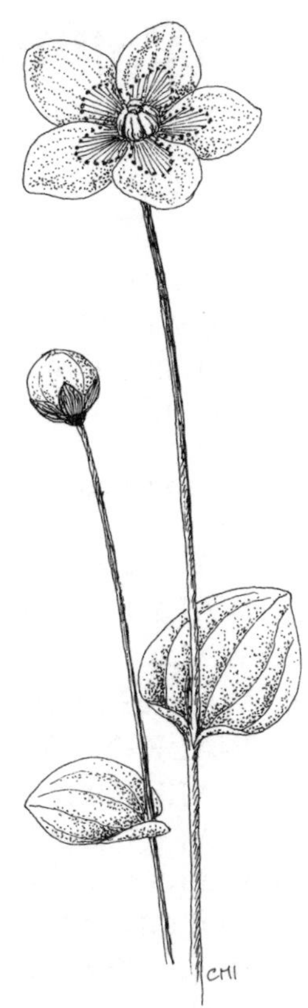

Grass of Parnassus

Practicals

Type of walk: This is another fine walk around Coll's lovely coastline. It is mostly on paths but easy walking when not.

Total Distance:	1½ miles/2km
Time:	1–2 hours depending on time spent bird watching etc.
Maps:	OS Explorer 372/Landranger 46

Walking Scotland Series
from
Clan Books

MARY WELSH has already compiled walkers' guides to each of the areas listed; material for guides covering the remaining parts of Scotland is being gathered for publication in future volumes.

Titles published so far:

1. WALKING THE ISLE OF ARRAN
2. WALKING THE ISLE OF SKYE
3. WALKING WESTER ROSS
4. WALKS IN PERTHSHIRE
5. WALKING THE WESTERN ISLES
6. WALKING ORKNEY
7. WALKING SHETLAND
8. WALKING THE ISLES OF ISLAY, JURA AND COLONSAY
9. WALKING GLENFINNAN: THE ROAD TO THE ISLES
10. WALKING THE ISLES OF MULL, IONA, COLL AND TIREE
11. WALKING DUMFRIES AND GALLOWAY
12. WALKING ARGYLL AND BUTE
13. WALKING DEESIDE, DONSIDE AND ANGUS
14. WALKING THE TROSSACHS, LOCH LOMONDSIDE AND THE CAMPSIE FELLS
15. WALKING GLENCOE, LOCHABER AND THE GREAT GLEN